CONTENTS

Published by
Dog Horn Publishing
45 Monk Ings, Birstall, Batley WF17 9HU
United Kingdom
doghornpublishing. com

Edited by
Garrett Cook
& Chris Kelso

Advertising Enquiries:
chris@doghornpublishing.com

'Mayor Nimble Makes it Known' by Steve Aylett,
first published in Alan Moore's *Dodgem Logic*.
Reprinted with permission of the author.

Distribution: **Central Books**
99 Wallis Road, London, E9 5LN, United Kingdom
orders@centralbooks. com
Phone:+44 (0) 845 458 9911
Fax: +44 (0) 845 458 9912

OUT NOW:
WOMEN WRITING THE WEIRD
EDITED BY DEB HOAG

RRP: £14.99 ($28.95). ISBN: 9781907133268, 216pp, trade paperback

featuring
Nancy A. Collins, Eugie Foster, Janice Lee, Rachel Kendall, Candy Caradoc, Mysty Unger, Roberta Lawson, Sara Genge, Gina Ranalli, Deb Hoag, C. M. Vernon, Aliette de Bodard, Caroline M. Yoachim, Flavia Testa, Aimee C. Amodio, Ann Hagman Cardinal, Rachel Turner, Wendy Jane Muzlanova, Katie Coyle, Helen Burke, Janis Butler Holm, J.S. Breukelaar, Carol Novack, Tantra Bensko, Nancy DiMauro, and Moira McPartlin.

The Imperial Youth Review
Issue 1

INTRODUCTION THE FIRST:
Union Jacks and Vespas and
Doctor Who and Whatnot
Garrett Cook

William the Conqueror. *Imperial Youth Review.* Shakespeare. *Imperial Youth Review.* The Beatles. *Imperial Youth Review.* Monty Python. *Imperial Youth Review.* Black Sabbath. *Imperial Youth Review.* The Sex Pistols. *Imperial Youth Review.* I have just listed for you, with no immodesty whatsoever, the most important British things ever. Britain, I believe this publication will be the thing that makes Americans finally forgive you for the whole taxation without representation thing. And India finally forgive you for Amritsar. It's okay, Britain. I'll call it even for all of the other cool things listed above.

When Chris Kelso approached me to edit *The Imperial Youth Review*, I was excited. Then Dog Horn got involved and I became ecstatic. "Hundred Year Old Murders" , my first story in print, was published in Issue 3 of Dog Horn's fantastic journal *Polluto*. It was about Jack the Ripper, another of Britain's favourite sons. So Dog Horn's always done right by me. Not to mention Dog Horn publisher Adam Lowe trusted us enough to let this be our vision.

I told Chris I wanted this magazine to be what would happen if Forrest Ackerman and Malcolm McLarenwoke up together in an alley after a drinking binge and invented *The New Yorker*. Because fuck *The New Yorker*. We're young and hip and deadly. We chased down most of the coolest cats and kitties we knew to do our damnedest to make sure you're reading that magazine and if you don't feel you're reading it yet, give it time. We'll get there together.

So, tally-ho and allons-y, I wanna be . . . anarchy! Enjoy *Video Watchdog* editor and *Throat Sprockets* author Tim Lucas' first short story in print, a heartfelt story that makes straight edge punk as fuck by Edward Morris, a new Christmythos story by Nick Mamatas and Don Webb, an essay on calligraphy by Tom Bradley, magic lessons, pulp artwork and more. This is *The Imperial Youth Review*. Some of it is British.

Some people call Garrett Cook a space cowboy. But not twice. Don't you look at me! I mean him. Bizarro author, scientist, sorcerer, lothario. Garrett Cook is many things to many people. He edits this magazine, so that's something. His books include the Murderland *series,* Archelon Ranch *and* Jimmy Plush, Teddy Bear Detective. *Both of the last two were nominated for the Wonderland Award for excellence in bizarro fiction. He is a singer/songwriter for the band Mayonnaise Jenkins and the Former Kings of the Delta Blues, whose album* A Monday *will be available for digital download by the time this magazine comes out and will be available on CD sometime later. He is not British, but he fucking bloody well is, so if you got a problem with that, let your Wilkinson do the talking, you fucking ponce!*

INTRODUCTION THE SECOND:
INVITATION TO A BEHEADING
Chris Kelso

This publication, without lofty threat of false advertising, will change your life forever.

– BUY THIS MAGAZINE! –

Compelled by a vivid dream I had one night about a quality literary/culture magazine full of totally amazing shit, I promptly quite my day job as a librarian and set out on a mission to make it a reality.

When attempting to assemble the *Imperial Youth Review*, I knew I could never accomplish it alone—you see, I can barely dress myself without help from some sort of geriatric nursing aide.

– GO ON THEN, BUY IT! –

In an effort to find my spiritual collaborator, I engaged in dialogue with all kinds of people. Some enlightening, some less so.

But I needed guidance.

– IT CURES CANCER! –

First, I ambled with a tribe of contemporary nomads based in the highlands, leading the pastures herd and living out of a communal caravan. Following a couple of day's integration, I was convinced to participate in an ancient tradition of bloodletting—apparently everyone does it these days.

I had been promised all would become clear as crystal quartz after the ceremony—the eagerness to uncover my illusive dream-brother meant I was more willing than usual to try new things.

– CURES BALDNESS TOO –

This ultimately ended with me shedding almost a litre of my own viscera, passing out in a field then waking up the next morning with no pants on and a wallet stripped of all its contents.

So.

– MAKES YOU SERIOUSLY IRRESISTIBLE TO WOMEN, SERIOUSLY! –

Not to be deterred, I sought residency in a Tibetan monastery where I recited numerous Buddhist incantations, pledged my soul to religious asceticism and found an inner solitude I had not tasted since my childhood.

However, I did NOT find my fucking collaborator.

I searched everywhere for a sign—from Moscow to Cambodia, Sarajevo to Timbuktu. I eventually returned to Scotland—forlorn, wandering the desolate streets of a capital city as vast, lonely and complex as circles in Dante's Hell.

– MAKES SENSE OF LIFE'S VAGUENESS –

I had already knotted the noose tightly around my neck and mounted the stack of bucket chairs, fully accepting my punishment for a mission failed, when suddenly I saw a silhouette in the doorway.

– ELIMINATES PERSONAL UNCERTAINTY –

Garrett Cook—just standing there with a ginormous set of garden shears in his hands.

He cut me down, slapped me in the face twice with the back of his hairy hand and told me he'd been sent to help. He told me he'd had the same dream I had and that meditating deeply brought him here.

"I'm from the city of Roses and extinct volcanos on its outskirts. Now pick yourself up and put on a clean pair of underwear. We've got a revolution to start motherfucker."

I had no idea an American would be sent?

– SEND US ALL YOUR MONEY –

So there you go. This is actually how it happened—the noble story of *Imperial Youth Review*. Our message is equally noble. Tell your friends.

– IF YOU DON'T BUY THIS, TERRORISTS WILL MURDER YOU –

Enjoy!

Chris Kelso is a writer, illustrator, editor and journalist from Scotland. His first short story collection Schadenfreude *is to be released by Dog Horn Publishing, while two of his other books have already been sold to publishers. Chris's work can be found in various anthologies and literary/arts magazines.* chris-kelso. com

I WILL REFUSE
Edward Morris

Words. Words. Words. I remember words, when there were people around who could still say words. Sometimes the ones who come can remember a few. Mostly, they leave me alone. The crawling chaos, the further-gone undead who come in the night to den here, smell something off in me. Something off in the meat, the meat, the meat that remains.

I am a patient boy. I wait in this back parlor room with two walls made out of windows, where the light's fairly bright at any time of day. We're high on a hill. There's a tree, and a river far below.

I sit in durance vile, and wait out this war. Life is an illusion. This all looks like a dream. I want to step out of my skin, but I'm scared to see what's beneath it. I'm scared.

I weathered worse than this in life, watching it all come down. I wait. It's been a while. I got bitten a long time ago. Days. This all feels like a dream. Like someone else's worst nightmare.

I beat the crawlers off with an aluminum Louisville slugger I filled with QuikRete once after a water run, and left to set. Dead or alive, anything that gets hit that many times with my toy doesn't walk for long. I still won't touch my food. Not my food. Didn't choose it. Won't eat dead things. Won't. Eat. Never would.

And for the love of all that is intelligent within the human species, I wouldn't make myself zombie-stupid when I was alive. The X tattooed on the back of my hand doesn't wash off. The X from Belmont Avenue in Chicago. The X that means a chemical no one but me can produce. The X that means Straight Edge. I cannot numb out now. Live or dead, tats don't come off. Cannot now. Refuse. Refuse. Refuse.

I smell radiation in the air, thick as metal. I hear it burning in the ground. I hear it killing what could be my food. Really no sign of a cease-fire, out there outside the window where everything is smoke and blood. I watched two living soldiers saw an Undead in half. One of them was enjoying it way too much. The other worked way too quickly not to have had the practice.

I've seen tanks, flame-tracks, all manner of nastiness. They used white phosphorous. UN statutes fall short of protecting the living-impaired, I can only assume.

But the firefights have gotten farther apart. There's that. I can still sleep. I can still meditate. Just like in jail after a protest, or stuck in an MRI, or any other place where you know, like my Buddhist friends say, that the breath has ceased in your lungs and you once again sit in the presence of the Divine.

I hear what could be my food, dying, dying, dying out there in the mud and the radiation. But I won't go out and eat any of them. I won't eat. I won't. I will resist.
I will refuse. Every time I get hungry, I make myself remember. I keep telling myself every damn little bit of my life before this non-life-Lite, grasping for names or faces like straws in a maelstrom. Sometimes they come. I write them down. I weave them into a web, a timeline of who we were and what we did. My Katie and me. My folks. My sisters. Everyone I can think of.
I draw their faces, when I can remember. I hope I spelled their names right. I hope. I hope I don't damage the page, as I change. But I can only change so long, before I'm free.
The walking dead won't waste shells on me, because I beg them to every time I see one or two or more of them. They smell me and they can tell that I refuse to eat.
Eat. I Have. Refused. To eat. Since something took a chunk out of me. In that, I have not wavered. I will refuse. I will resist. I will resign. I. Will. And Will alone.
Until I die again.
I have to die again.

I can still sleep. I can still appreciate sleep, in my little room with the radio-TV and the blankets and books and blank notebooks, the pencils worn to stubs, the notebooks graven to shiny gray relief.
The cigar boxes advising REOROI-TAN: THE CIGAR THAT BREATHES to a twice-dead world where there are neither Roi-Tans nor re-orders. The magazines that just look funnier and funnier. The pocketknife. The pile of shavings, arranged into what looks like a mandala. The dead monitor, and TV. And me.

The thing that helps the most is when I write about the hard parts. The easy parts are like newspaper. Like snowflakes. The hard parts make me feel alive.

Holding Katie in my arms the first night we really ever slept together. Not fucked. Slept together. People don't make the distinction. The first night we ever held each other until the birds got loud and the sun came up and we told each other everything we thought we still didn't know.
When I found myself with two big sleeve-tattooed armfuls of weeping girl, as she hacked up the chainsaw-massacre of what it was like to grow up the youngest

7

daughter in a family-owned slaughterhouse. "Some things, "she finally managed, her voice gradually growing less raspy, "Some things, David, you believe because of what you see. Because once you see something, you can't believe anything else."

I remember some of the things I saw. Some of the footage. All the places are different, but the footage is the same: The factory chickens with no beaks, fat and blind in the dark, their babies threshed when they mistakenly hatched

Every Cowschwitz waist-deep in ditch-liquor, every pig beaten with a tire iron on every security camera. All the years. Everything people walked right by because it didn't happen in their backyard, and everything that came with that, all the parasites that fed on behaviors we should have evolved out of a long time ago. Making the world a sweatshop. Criminalizing the creative class. Eating meat. Any meat at all.

Any. Meat. At. All. It'd be better to die right now. I would lose my senses beneath the infection, let my soul float right on out the door when no one was looking, maybe, if.

But there's no such thing as Death. Not anymore. Not since Friday. What day is it now? Tuesday. I think. Outside this ruined house, the last of the shelling stopped on Monday.

Wait. Monday. I remember that. Monday. The soldiers had radios. They were undead. Undead with radios. I almost cared.

Wait. Radios. What were radios? Everybody out there was moving. Moving. Movingmovingmoving and I could hear

I could hear, between the music, the voice telling what day it was, telling me: ARMED FORCES RADIO STATION IDENTIFICATION MONDAY JANUARY TEN, TWENTY THIRTEEN, UNDER THE AEGIS OF THE SECOND CONSTITUTIONAL CONVENTION AND COMMANDER IN CHIEF GENERAL ELEANOR BISHOP. THE TIME IS NOW PRECISELY

No such thing as Time. No such thing as Death any more. The soldiers didn't come find me. Neither kind. I yelled and yelled, but they made like they didn't hear.

Living soldiers are all the same. I come up to them and beg for a bullet. Because I beg they laugh. They've been through a lot. Letting me live probably makes them feel like real big people, while they torture someone who used to be one of them.

"That one will die on its own, "some puffed-up empty uniform of a lieutenant said two feet from my face, six months and change ago when I dropped the water-bucket and began my spiel at the deaf, blistered ears of two raw recruits. I could see the officer seeing the way I was dressed, the straight-edge X tattooed on the back of my left hand from when I was still alive.

"I don't think you really believe that, "I told him back. And that scared him stiff. Mostly, the soldier saw that he was in trouble, because even undead, I saw further into him than he could into me. He couldn't hack the look in my eyes that said I was trying not to see red, but still remembered what Government meant, and still had no use for it deep down.

"Hey, look, "he chuckled, "This was one of those Oh, what did they call 'em "He makes the incredible intellectual leap of memory, "Straight edgers. Like, Punk rockers, but they don't take drugs or fuck or "The chuckle grew louder. "Bet he didn't even eat meat. "He looked at me like he was talking to me. "Time to chow down, punkerfaggot. Somebody else'll settle your hash."

Then they just walked away. If I could have run fast enough, I would have torn the bastard's throat out.

But I wouldn't.

Because some things are just a part of you, and it is those things you know you'd defend to the death, whether or not anyone ever asked you. Some things apparently even outlast the great misnomer I used to call Death.

Some things, you just have to believe, no matter what the world is or isn't doing all around you, because when you comprehend what you've seen with your own two eyes, it becomes impossible to see the world any other way.

Some vows you can't just go back on when you feel like it.

I remember Dad dropping that buck at a dead run. I remember him unzipping its belly.

I remember just sitting down, resisting passively. Sitting down on that rock, with my jaw somewhere near my breastbone. I knew I wouldn't cry. I was too sick to cry, and I wouldn't give the old man the satisfaction of calling me a faggot to my face. Kids who have to be little grownups learn quick. Comes with the gig.

So I got up and helped. I held my breath and I helped, and when I got home I took the longest shower that Mom ever heard anyone take, she said. She looked at me a long time, but never asked.

I told the deer in the freezer that I was sorry. And that it'd never happen again.

It didn't.

Sometimes the radio weaves every note of every military broadcast of martial music and atrocious antediluvian glam-rock to shock and awe the enemy into auditory submission, all of those blur into a single thread, a single note that becomes a clear light.

I sleep, sometimes. Did I say that? Believe it or not. I sleep. Sleep. Sleep calls me out of the top of my head, to come along the silver cord, back to our true home.

Beyond the dead world of the living and the middle world of the zombie, into a different space where things hold cosmic vastness, where perspectives and points of view change with dizzying speed.

Calling me back to our True Home.

I don't know how much longer I can hold a pencil, but that's okay. I'm running out of paper. Thank you for reading this

far

I can't get

up any more. Time moves

like foul humors down a

drain. I am patient. I wait.

and

wait.

(For David Agranoff)

Edward Morris is a 2011 nominee for the Pushcart Prize in Literature, also nominated for the 2009 Rhysling Award and the 2005 British Science Fiction Association Award. His short fiction has appeared almost a hundred times worldwide so far, most recently in Joseph Pulver's A Season in Carcosa, *Trent Zelazny's* Mirages *and (forthcoming)* The Lovecraft Ezine. *Look for his rebooted series* There was a Crooked Man, *due out from Mercury Retrograde Press this fall.*

BANISHTON
Tim Lucas

You can never go back to Banishton, but there is a voice as enticing as any siren's song, heard at odd hours on the radio, beckoning you back there. You can also find this voice on records, dating from a time when you were more available and your life more adventurous; nowadays, those records are hard to find and, even if you should happen to remember the name of the artist, none of today's shops have heard of the singer or her music. Yet her voice wends through your memory, plucking a guilty response, impossible to play except in memory. You're half-convinced the record is a product of your own imagination until the day comes when you finally see it in the cheap vinyl racks peering back at you, buried between inconsequence and inconsequence. Holding the record in your hands at last—with its splitting cardboard sleeve, inscribed on the back with the name of someone you might have known in Banishton—you struggle to restrain the violence of awakened emotions, holding back the tears that prove you weren't crazy to believe it existed, that it once was, and then, tenderly, you put it backrealizing that, to own it, to bring it into your life now, to listen to it as obsessively as you know you will, will prompt unwelcome questions. So you leave it there, you return to your car and you drive, drive on, drive anywhere—except to Banishton.

After the time you spent in Banishton, you returned home but not as you were. You returned a divided person, the exact moment of rift visible in the extensions of the centermost cross in the palm of your hand, the hand you use to write. You know that you are not alone in how you feel. You have seen other men like you; they haunt airports late at night, holding no tickets, their eyes intent upon the arrivals and departures, looking on covetously at the hellos and goodbyes of strangers, their faces furrowed with ashen longing. You have seen women in airport bars desperate to drown these mewling emotions, in dance if not in drink, but mostly in drink; you have engaged a few in conversation and they confided in you, being a stranger, that no matter how many Cosmos or Dirty Martinis they imbibed, they knew they could not resist any man who might sit next to them and flash two tickets to Banishton. But that man is not you, you have your reasons, you tell them, as you step away.

Look as you might, you will never find a spinning rack of postcards tempting tourists to Banishton, no color view of its skyline fogged-in with the ghosts of nostalgic visitors. Its portals are closed, its towers darkened with shades lowered to half-mast, its terminals terminated. Its streets are a place where people find themselves accidentally, suddenly in way over their heads, involved in compromising ventures consummated in whispers and inevitable tears. It's inaccessible, but the unexpected sound of that voice, laughing from the car with Banishton plates that speeds past you on the open highway, can accelerate the beating of your heart as your car slows to a sudden crawl. Then you must regather yourself and step on the gas, eyes trained on the license plates scattered around you like so many business cards, but you've lost the one you so desperately seek in all that traffic. You surrender and check the oncoming exit signs for all-night diners, bars that look like they can keep a secret, or perhaps the airport. Sometimes, unable to forget that brief encounter, you may find yourself climbing back into your car in the middle of the night, accelerating with hope but no clear intent in the direction of no known destination, looking for familiar turn-offs in your twin-barreled headlights. Your throat feels parched with all those goodbyes you once said in Banishton, under awnings, under rainfall, under the deep duress of departure. You feel you might be getting closer, the farther you edge forth into unknown darkness, and you begin to recall more details of that other place and time. They rise to the surface out there in the dark of the rural flatlands, threatening to collide with you like a thrill-seeker speeding through the night with his beacons set to black, but passing through you with a dry stammer of regret that beckons you on. You drive till morning, all the turn-offs behind you left untaken, finally returning to the woman with whom you share your life, though actually very little of your inner life, chuckling out a bemused explanation they don't believe but somehow patiently accept, about how you were out driving all night because you couldn't sleep.

Your loved ones, those with whom you are most intimate, have never heard of Banishton. Banishton, whose bordering lakes are the colors of the ice in your double Tanquerey, as the cubes spin like the scraps of an exploded world around your stirring finger. If you could only leave the booze alone, you tell yourself, you might find the strength of character to forget or deny Banishton, and the way your time spent there forever changed you. No one else has seen the change; it hasn't quite registered in their senses, but it's real. It's real and more the totality of you than the person they think they know, the stranger who takes their love and never opens up—because that's the way they do things in Banishton.

The people you left behind in Banishton sometimes call you, their distant voices raw with familiarity, a familiarity by which you feel slightly embarrassed to still be known after all this time. They target your furtive heart, these out-of-the-blue communications, some of them tinged with urgency or enticement, because they remind you that Banishton continues to exist without you. The stores and bars, the streets you once frequented, they still endure, selling their cigarettes, dispensing their liquor, picking up people of whose beauty you dare not dream in their buses. Days go by there, without you enjoying the company of these persistent phantoms, observing their routine, without you being there, revelling in its residents and places before they die or are torn down. Your old friends say they miss you, but somehow it's not the same when they pass through town and come to visit. It's not like it was when you were in Banishton with them, spilling your heart on their living room floors late at night, embarrassing yourself in irreparable ways to be truthful, so far from your own friends and family that you came to the realization of who you are, could only come to that realization outside the reach of their shaping influence. They were with you when you heard her voice for the first time; they have all of her records in Banishton, of course they remember that record, they know all her songs, including some you haven't heard, some that might serve to further unlock your heart, and it is a certainty that they listen to them without you—especially the new one. Yes, there's a new one. They call to see if you've heard it, to let you know that her new songs reminded them of you, of the time you were there, and made them all very aware of how much you are missed back in Banishton.

You hang up the phone and look at your possessions, all the comforts you have acquired in your life, thirty years ago or just last week, and you resent the weight of them as they crowd and threaten to crush the life out of you. You think about selling everything you own, about letting all your baggage go, making you weightless, irresponsible, free to return once again to Banishton but all the roads of fantasy converge upon a central plaza of practicality. Once you reach it, you realize that the money you received in kind would hold you down just as much, if not more. You ask yourself if you have the strength to simply pick up and go to leave your soiled clothes in the hamper, the unread books on your shelves, the dirty dishes in the sink, your plasma screen plugged into the wall, and run for your life down the open road. But the answer is no, so a black sliver in your thought of thoughts causes you to wish in your heart of hearts that someone staking out the neighborhood would come and rob you, sometime when you are out of the house, leaving you with nothing but the clothes on your back, the clothes of your return, the clothes you wore that last night you were in Banishton.

The photos you took in Banishton, the ones you hide at the back of a drawer, have begun to fade—not their colors, but their significance—and this worries you. You used to stare at one or two of them every opportunity you could steal, until they made your life so painful it could not be endured; so you hid them away—more from yourself than from your wife, or from anyone else. Finding yourself thinking about Banishton again, and why you can never return there, you turn to these pictures for some account of the past and find the images strangely unyielding, indifferent to your probing gaze in ways they never were before. You wonder who these people are and how they ever could have touched you so deeply. Who are these strangers—the ones who still call, the ones to whom you never spoke? How did these satellites of your existence acquire the power to threaten your life, to fill you with such fear?

You have hundreds of videos, hundreds of channels, so many hundreds of albums at your disposal, yet you peruse your sagging shelves for hours, desperate for diversion, finding none of it up to the task of replacing Banishton in your mind. All these things represent your tastes, the very essence of the person you are, but not one of them, you realize, represents the person you were in Banishton. When they discover you in an abstract state, watching the rain from the swing in your solarium, or standing for no apparent reason on the roof of your house at midday, your family and friends ask with increasing concern what's on your mind. Money, the current headlines, the book you're pretending to read—these are the excuses you grab from thin air when people catch you lost in thoughts of Banishton.

You've been on a health kick for years, you've lost sixty pounds, but this voice recalled from Banishton seduces you back into some of your old bad habits. What a pleasant surprise, even a coincidence, it seems when you find those Egyptian cigarettes you used to smoke in Banishton at a local tobacconist. They cost a bit more than the cigarettes sold in all the convenience stores, but you like the oval shape of them and pay for them as you would pay for a plane ticket, feeling like a citizen of the world, knowing full well that you would have paid up to the price of a plane ticket for the privilege of inhaling these, as close as you dare come to filling your senses with the forbidden sights and sounds and smells of Banishton. You can't resist lighting one up before leaving the shop, too eager for this sensory blossoming to wait, too hungry for the inevitable disorientation that comes halfway through the pack, when you begin to wonder why the reality of Banishton should be forever barred to you.

The subject of buying a new house arises over dinner one night, and you resist the idea, which would be tantamount to signing a contract obliging you to stay in this life you scarcely inhabit. There is also the troubling notion that a relocation would move you one step away from the one place where your past knows it can find you, should it ever have need or want of you. You want to remain accessible to the past, though you know that availability can never go both ways. To be agreeable, and to avoid explanations and the scene that you fear would occur if you told your wife how you really feel, you go with her to look at a series of houses within your budget—one of them, vacated by an older woman who has succumbed to her final illness, retains a sickly atmosphere but you resist it less than those houses that extend themselves to you in a manner that feels too welcoming. You can sense the bonds that tie you to Banishton hardening around your heart as you test the wall-to-wall carpeting, the views from the windows and balconies. You ask yourself if this isn't what you really need: a carpet soft enough beneath your feet to allow your roots to sink down, deep enough to permanently erase the possibility of taking another leave from your human equation.

The owners take you by surprise when they accept your low-ball offer, as eager to embrace their own future in another city, a city nearer to Banishton, as you are to know where you stand and with whom. It is a hardship but you move, knowing that the difficulties will only increase if you wait until you are older and more settled in your disappointments. You move, but not far enough away that your telephone number changes; your Banishton friends continue to call, disturbing you, shattering your stray moments of happiness, reeling you back into that most wonderful hurt, reminding you of dramas and dreams you had almost forgotten. They tell you how poorly they are bearing up in Banishton without you, that they miss you; they urge you to come back, wondering innocently and aloud why you refuse to budge, why you have opted out of their lives. They assure you that no one remembers your embarrassment, the vulnerable exhibition you made of yourself, and then they add that those who do have long since forgiven you—after all, we're all human. After all, we've all been there. You give them some new stories about yourself to spread about town, so the right people of Banishton might remember you, the ones who never call, and smile at the reminder of your name, if it means anything to them at all. They remind you, these sudden callers, that their doors are always open, that the futon is still there in the study, awaiting you. They don't seem to understand that all your old bridges have been burned, just as you don't really understand how that match came to be ignited, or why it still burns.

In your new home, you discover that the only wax capable of blocking your ears from the siren song of Banishton is manual labor. The house needs some modest repairs and you address yourself to these: pinning the stonework around your foundation, caulking the windows that rattle in high winds, rainproofing the porches and patio. You rake the dead leaves from your yellowing lawns in autumn, shovel snow off your driveway in winter, replace some missing slates from your roof in spring, and swim off your frustrations with laps in the neighbor's pool during those summer months where the grounds seem to take care of themselves, except for the lawns mowed by the neighbor's teenage son, all the while whistling tunes whose names you can't remember, but which somehow pitch a champion wind into your sails. Sitting with your wife on your patio, looking with some righteous satisfaction over a slice of the world that the two of you call your own, whilst divvying up the rest of the world between his and hers, you fish your packet of Egyptian cigarettes out of your shirt pocket. Thoughtfully, you reseat yourself downwind of her, knowing she can't stand the smell of them—or is it what she fears they represent? Lighting up, your thoughts dance and spark to the cadence of one of the songs you've whistled while you work; then it advances from your subconscious to consciousness, boldly disclosing itself to you like the significance of the cards you turn over when your sister-in-law gives you one of her Thanksgiving tarot readings. Yes, it was another song you heard for the first time in Banishton. This comes as no surprise, but it was not one of those you call the siren songs. At once, you remember exactly where you were when you first heard it, and with whom. It was playing on the jukebox in a Country Kitchen as the two of you talked, making promises neither of you had any intention of keeping; it was a neighborhood fixture, that place, the underside of your booth table pimpled with wads of petrified bubble gum stuck there by bobby-soxers in the 1940s and the sock-hoppers of the 1950s. There was coffee on the table that night, two cups of hot coffee; you recall that you had been a tea drinker until you came to Banishton. The unbidden memory of the Country Kitchen awakens an urgent hankering for one of their hamburgers—the Country Boy, it was called—it's something you haven't tasted in many years—something no one has tasted in many years, because the last of the Sixty Second Shops closed its doors for all eternity long ago. Another irrecoverable taste tied to the barred gates of Banishton. To quell these troubled appetites, you pour yourself a drink—it might be a cognac, perhaps some mezcal with the worm, anything but the Campari and orange juice that for awhile was your drink of choice in Banishton.

At home you are silent, you listen as others speak, and yet, during the time you visited Banishton, you remember that you were something of an extrovert. You smile at the memory of the party where you charmed so many strangers by describing yourself as a recreational liar. It was a good opening, wasn't it? How it intrigued the other guests as you stood there, in the middle of a rich stranger's living room, smiling and holding court in a room to which you could never in a million years find your way back. You explained, speaking with animated hand gestures, that a recreational liar was not to be confused with a common liar—that is to say, someone who lies to save himself from inconvenience, to sidestep punishment, or to flatter himself. A recreational liar, you explained, limited his deceptions to those untruths that served only to enhance life. The men smiled, kittenish women arched their thinly strapped shoulders; everyone warmed to the idea and asked for examples. You told them that, if you happened to walk to the store and back home again and nothing happened, and if your partner later asked if anything interesting happened during your walk, you found it amusing to invent little ornamentation to make the laborious recounting of your ordinary walk less ordinary. At least half the crowd that gathered around you laughed and admitted to doing the same thing, and as you said your goodbyes, you collected the business cards of perhaps a dozen new friends at the end of the evening. You all promised that you would keep in touch, but—recreational liar that you were and are—you never did.

At another party, you introduced yourself as a Gemini—a Gemini whose most important friendships in childhood all happened to be with twins. They are all gone from your life now, those early friends, but you remain a Gemini through and through, and sometimes wonder if it is the divided nature of your zodiac sign

16

that is responsible for your persistent desire to always be somewhere else. Even in Banishton, you admit to yourself as you refresh your glass, your thoughts were always of the airport, of getting back home.   This passing thought triggers another, of the time when one of your closest friends moved away, of the time he came to you and explained how and why he had to find a life for himself in another city. He said that he couldn't bear to drive the streets of your city as an adult because they were the same streets he drove as a teenager, the streets where he had broken the speed limit, where he had driven without a license, where he had once driven under the influence and crashed into a parked vehicle. Here he drove the streets of old collisions and collusions, like a ghost, and they made him pine for a place where he could drive without passing through other ghosts at every intersection. You realise, as you mull over these things he said, that this city, where you continue to live, is his Banishton.

In the dusk, the trees behind the house you share form a black lace enclosure against a slate black sky, and you remind yourself that there's a white house that you've strengthened inside this shell. It knows you, this place, your strengths and limitations can be read in the driving of every rafter nail. It has kept you able, stable and out of trouble, this place, a bubble of containment too sound to pop. On the day you drop, your house may mourn you, but no less inscrutably than the sky weeps when clouds burst and rain falls hard. The true measure of your loss, you tell yourself, can be calculated only by the number of black envelopes responding to its announcement, each and every one of them postmarked Banishton.

Your wife continues to sit beside you in the waning light. She casts her private gaze into the distance, at the skyline of your city as it freckles with luminance, unaware of that internal place where yours has drifted once again. It's the gentle squeezing of her hand, reaching over from the yellow armrest of her lawn chair, you realize, that makes yours real. You answer "no" when she asks if you'll be going out. She murmurs her approval and, feeling like some music, reaches for the radio.

Tin Lucas is the author of two novels, Throat Sprockets *(1994) and* The Book of Renfield: A Gospel of Dracula *(2005), hard copies of which can still be found online, and which are coming soon as ebooks. His critical biography* Mario Bava: All the Colors of the Dark *(2007), won the International Horror Guild Award, the Saturn Award for Special Achievement and the Independent Publishers Award. "Banishton" is his first published short story.*

AND OTHER HORRORS
Don Webb/Nick Mamatas

It was the third jittery day. The job was supposed to be simple. Bob, Frank and Reg stole the truck, Sam would meet them and buy the cigarettes. Then they would be sold at bars and clubs in Memphis. Places that didn't look too closely at the tax stickers. Bob was too old and too smart for this kind of thing, but as the saying goes "bills to pay and mouths to feed." They parked the stolen truck behind the Pine Lodge. Frank smeared some mud over the license as though that rendered the eighteen-wheeler invisible. Frank and Reg were neither too young nor too stupid for this sort of job. In fact, Bob decided they weren't too stupid for anything. They remained drunk, living on delivered pizza in their increasingly rank room on the second floor. Beer, cigarettes, pizza and hotel porn were for them a sort of paradise, if not the "good life" a damn reasonable facsimile.

Bob stood in the parking lot watching the cars whiz by. He had Sam on the phone. Sam was about to bug out, "I don't know Bob, the feds have checked up on us twice this week. My money man is getting nervous."

"Do you want the fucking cigarettes or not? I am setting here with two drunks on the verge of flipping out on me. My ass is totally exposed."

"Maybe we can cut a deal for less money."

"Maybe you can go to hell."

"Why don't you just cut them out of it? You drive into town tomorrow night, I'll give my share of the money and you blow the state for awhile."

"If do that these jokers will show up at my house and kill me. They may not be smart but they are vicious."

"I'm going to see what I can do. Think abut my offer, and Bob you should have some plans to get out of Dodge. No one is watching out for you."

Fuck this shit.

At least he had his car here. All the two morons had was the truck. He walked into the front office. They could drink cheap and jerk off in the bathroom of room 2D forever. The fat hippy chick with greasy long (maybe) blonde hair was watching the tube. A tiny fake Christmas tree stood on the counter. The place smelled of cheap cone incense that almost covered the smell of pot. Place probably didn't have a cashbox. Her red eyes were a neon advertisement for Don't Do Drugs. Probably hadn't had a thought in years. The TV babbled on—one of those popular shows about the paranormal. Seemed to be more of that crap every year. What was this one? Bewildering Balderdash, Spooky Situations, Ripley's Believe It Or Don't, In Search of Grainy Stock Footage? Currently the narrator was describing the case of Bob Sturges, a New York construction worker. As the black and white photo

18

showed, Bob had fallen on a long piece of rebar from the unfinished tenth floor of the Empire State Building. Although the rebar had pierced Bob through his right eye and up through and out of his skull. He had survived. His fast-thinking foreman had cut Bob loose (as seen in the photo) and took him to a nearby physician's office. Someone had thought to make this photo while Bob was waiting to see the doctor. It didn't help Bob's mood that he shared the name with that guy.

"What do you think of that?" asked hippy chick. She wore a somewhat faded Joker T-Shirt with the bloody line Why So Serious? across the tits. Bob searched for a deep sounding come back in hope of scoring some of the dope or maybe some hippy pussy.

"I believe everything happens for a reason." he said. That should work, these people believe in karma.

She made a disgusted face, like she had just found a rat turd in her cereal. She slightly nodded her head no as she responded, "Typical answer. Mister you ever think that there might be a force in the universe that intervenes for the opposite reason? A force that makes things happen precisely for no reason? Look around sometime."

"Yeah, well you got me there."

Bob left the office. The manager could continue her advanced nihilism. Bob just wanted to go. She stayed in the unit behind the office. He walked over. Dusk had come and he needed to have something to show for the risks of the last three days. No one was around, he pulled a broken case cutter from his jeans pocket and jimmied open the door. Stepped in and closed it behind him. First goal was the kitchenette. He needed a garbage sack. Done. DVD Player. Laptop. Cheap shit but something. In the bedroom an over-sized vibrator that looked like Godzilla—it was called Ain't Love Grand? Some cheap turquoise and silver jewelry. Hard and smooth; real turquoise feels soapy to the touch. Bingo! A baggy filled with weed. Her books. Paranormal romances, several books about freak accidents, and a Bible.

No it wasn't a Bible. Something old in a light brown cover, a book of poetry. Azathoth and Other Horrors by Edward Pickman Derby. Probably not worth squat. But it did look old. Into the bag. "I'll show you what happens for no reason." he said to the room and cat-footed it out like a fog to his green Camry. He put the loot, such as it was, in the passenger seat. Let Frank and Reg deal with a truck that grew hotter by the minute.

He didn't head home. He headed toward Clearlake. His cousin would buy the crap off of him and he could hit town next week. By then some suitable entanglement would have overtaken the boys and he could be looking for a new job legit or not. Frank was so stupid that he'd put the room on his credit card. Bob's only interaction with the Pine Lodge had been the philosophical dialog and the manager hadn't even

19

looked fully away from the TV. If there had been a security camera he hadn't spotted it. She had probably removed it years ago to keep her ganga habit a secret. He turned off his cell phone.

He didn't want to drive all night to Clearlake. Damn near nothing on the road. How had Dad described it? "This road runs between nowhere and not much else. "Hadn't seen Dad much as a kid. He'd been a long-haul trucker. Maybe still was, or so Bob occasionally found himself thinking on the highways, when there was nobody on the road but commercial traffic. Bob's family had disowned him, or he them. Even his Uncle Robert Derby Sturges for whom he was named. Another meaningless coincidence. Not a star in sight. "Commercial traffic," Bob said. The stuff he'd lifted seemed to buzz at him, almost hopefully.

There was a truck stop ahead. He pulled in and parked in the back. He fished through the lot and got out the book. Bob loved to read, would've done well in college if hadn't been for selling speed on the side.

The book was signed, but not inscribed, which would add to its salability. A product of the Roaring Twenties. He ordered the scrambled eggs, ham, coffee biscuits and jelly. There were sequences of sonnets in the book describing a trip to the center of the cosmos, where pure Chaos sent out waves of senselessness, beauty-destroying asymmetry. Theses waves congealed into matter and energy and into gods of insane intent—vast cruel and perverse. Hell if this was your cosmos, drive-by shootings, the floating garbage island twice the size of Texas, John Wayne Gacy, and government subsidy of tobacco farming all made sense. For that matter so did he and Sam and Frank and Reg.

The food came. He put too much pepper on his eggs and poured the non-dairy creamer in the coffee. Some of the poems were scary, some really depressing, some black humor. Hell he might keep this book. Then he found a limerick:

> For the Daemon Sultan a chessman
> Reads my verse and finds the Plan
> A halfwit cousin, name of Sturges,
> Who loses and loses because of his urges.
> Repeats, Re-runs, Re-cycles as long as he can.

Limericks were supposed to be funny. This was not funny. This meaningless coincidence thread was wearying a little thin. He paid for his food and left. As he walked toward his car, he spied the passenger door ajar. Son of a bitch! Someone had stolen his ill-gotten goods. He slammed the door shut and pealed out of the parking lot. It seemed darker than before if that was possible. The darkness sucked at his headlights. After a couple of miles he saw a tanker truck coming his way. As

20

it grew closer he thought how clean it would feel to hit the truck and be purified by the fire. He started screaming to himself not to do it and fought his own crazy arms. He veered into the lane, the tanker blasted its horn and only at the last second did he pull back.

He peed himself. Bob could have sworn he heard a laugh track. For a moment he thought he saw vast forms in the darkness of the sky. They're blotting out the sky Maybe he was going crazy like his Uncle Robert had.

Bob decided he would stop at the next motel. Finally there it was The Oak Tree Lodge. A Xerox of the last motel, probably run by the same company. He pulled in front of the office. He had a fake credit card to secure the night.

The office looked the same. He quickly walked up to the counter to hide the pee spot on his jeans. Bob realized he was shaking. It seemed late at night, but it was really only nine. The clerk was a chubby woman wearing a faded T-shirt that advertised a punk band Erica Zann and the Electric Commode. She had dirty strawberry blonde hair that hung past her shoulders. She could have been the last chick's sister. The tiny Christmas tree could have come from the same fake tree farm—it bugged Bob, something about cones.

"Want a room?"

"Yeah."

He became aware of the TV. It showed a documentary about the increase of monster births. The manager said, "What do you think causes that?"

The screen showed a two-headed fetus.

Bob said, "I dunno but I think there may be a force that cause things to happen for precisely no reason. "He hoped the Force would notice in a good way.

The chick snorted. "Not too bad. I think it's the chemicals."

"The chemicals?"

"The government makes neurotoxins in Springfield—up the mile a stretch. We're going use it all on the Chinese some days. They ship 'em out in tanker trucks. One of the drivers told me one night. Makes me nervous so I smoke dope at night. Someday some halfwit will hit one of them and that's all she wrote."

"Yeah, got watch them halfwits."

"You 420-friendly?"

"Usually but tonight I am just dead tired."

"Well here's your card. Room 2D. It's around back. Merry Christmas, "she said, sliding the card over the counter. "Or is it happy holidays to you? "She rolled her eyes at herself.

Bob found the room. It reeked of Pall Malls, the sheets were damp. He put the Do Not Disturb card on the outside knob and put the chain on. He turned on every light in the room and he opened the book.

21

Choregos for Typhon's Play
The Egyptian ringmaster picks comedies both big and small
The other face of the Sultan wears many masks
Tonight's drama is about a larva's fall
Nyralathotep the other face of Azathoth does his many tasks
He breeds the maggots that call themselves men
And gives lesser lusts to each
He randomly scatters them upon Gaia's wide fen
And mad poets write trap-verses from them to teach
Look here comes one now unable to stop
Joining with the insects from Sgaggi's dance
That culls the weak under the black big top
Mutilating themselves in the Pharaoh's Trance
That which should crawl has learned to walk
And to add to the fun thinks it can Talk.

Eighty million years later, Bob looked up from the poem. The book was gone, and so too were Bob's limbs. What he looked down upon was not even remotely a human body. His torso was conic, more a trunk than anything else. He thought to touch it, but instead of an warm three great limbs—like rough ropes, but with the prehensility and subjective proprioception of fingers—swam into view. Bob jerked his head back. It was on another stalk and swung crazily. A huge library of sorts, other beings like him, conic and tentacled with a single huge eye. They lurched toward him.

Then, the hotel room again. Bob's clothes stuck to him. He felt clammy. He remembered suddenly that it was December, nearly Christmas. The chemicals, definitely. He reached for the remote and decided to turn on the television, for company. He wondered how Frank and Reg could do it, how they could just stumble through life like animals, eating anything that wandered into one end and excreting it out the other. Without a thought for the world. Bob realized that he was jealous. Television would help—it was like a lobotomy you could turn off when strictly necessary.

And they were on the TV, on the very first station he clicked on to. Frank and Reg, it looked like. They were on security camera footage the news was showing. Masked, Frank in some kind of shredded raincoat, flailing and waving his arms while kicking his way through a gas station window. Reg was almost catatonic, his hand up to his ear, probably on his stupid cell phone. Bob decided not to check his messages. The volume was low but by the time Bob had turned it up the news had already moved on to another story about some little girl caught in the crossfire between two rival gangs. She was dead. An altar with flowers and photos and flickering candles had already sprung up, but the police were baffled, the family enraged.

Bob knew he had to get moving again. Neither of his confederates would stay quiet even if they knew how to, and Bob wasn't anything but a four-time loser with a few greasy twenties in his pockets and a stolen book. Bob took a breath, decided to try to do something for no reason at all, bolted from the bed, realized the futility of trying to do something for no reason at all, and then ran from the room. He burst into the hall and then he was far too large for it, all stalk-limbs and a huge trunk. He flailed about in the body that wasn't his, slammed into the wall, stumbled backwards into the doorway of his room and landed flat on his back. The Do Not Disturb sign landed on his face.

Too late, Bob thought, disturbed.

Then the voice. Echoing in a head much larger than the head Bob remembered. "Nevil Kingston-Brown, cheers. William I in 1066. Hitler lost in 1945. Neil Armstrong first to the Moon in 1969. Flying polyps emerge in December 2012, eradicate most of the human race. Japan sinks 2121. First successful bilocation in 2357. Any of these ring a bell?"

A great spasm emerged from Bob's trunk as he tried to speak. The air was suddenly redolent with the smells of confusion and sexual release. Finally, Bob simply thought. "It is December 2012."

"It will be, "Bob heard in his head. "Well, that explains why you're here, now."

"Where?" Bob demanded. "When!"

"In the body of a member of the Great Race of Yith," Nevil said. "Some time in your past. Mine as well, actually. The Great Race have mastered the science of time travel. Hmm, no, that's not quite right. They have an acumen for it, and it's more of an art than a science. One of them—indeed, the one whose body you currently inhabit—is in your body on Earth, in December 2012. To watch the rise of the flying polyps and the eradication of most the human species and its multifarious cultures."

Bob didn't know what to say. Nothing in his experience had prepared him for even so odd a dream. For a moment, the thought why? bubbled to the surface of his suddenly very different feeling brain. But he didn't ask his question. He decided just to sit where he was, in the great and awkward hulk whose form he was growing used to—not as a body, but as a car a few days after stealing it, after the mirrors have been adjusted and the seat set back—and see what would happen if he did nothing.

After all, Bob thought, sometimes things happen for no reason.

"False," said Nevil. "All actions are caused actions. There is certainly no morality involved in even a single event, but actions have reasons for coming to pass.

23

If there is a problem at all, it is in comprehending the number of causes any event might have, not with the phony realization that 'things happen for no reason. '" Those last five words weren't in Nevil's voice, not with his rounded vowels and hissed consonants—they were in Bob's voice, like a recording, or a memory.

"Great, a philosopher," Bob's mind said. "Fine. How long will I be like this?"

"Until the being in your body has completed its observations. No time at all, really."

"And it's just me and you here now?"

Nevil didn't chuckle, but other voices, other minds, did. Thousands of them. Ancient men, older than civilization, whose forays into dark wisdom led to their predicaments. Things from other worlds, minds that can hardly have been said to have ever had bodies at all. Beetles with the minds of men and an academic knowledge of Bob's particular sort of ape, one long-extinct from their point of view. They weren't even laughing at the idea that he and Nevil would be alone, Bob realized, but at his use of the word now.

"You're not like us," Nevil said. "We're dreamers. Aesthetes. Our minds were open, one way or another, through art or science or thaumaturgy, made sensitive to the machinations of the Great Race. You may feel that the body you inhabit is a prison—"

"And you don't?" Bob said.

"I do," said Nevil. "But prisons aren't all of a type. Cooperate with the Great Race, and you'll gain access to a library beyond imagining. Dozens of worlds, tens of millions of years. Sciences both exoteric and esoteric. Forms of poetry our human bodies wouldn't even have the organs to appreciate. It's here for you Bob."

Bob felt the world around him snicker. He thought back to the book, the chaos of the evening. To poems he couldn't appreciate.

"I know a book," he said, finally. He wasn't addressing Nevil, but the assembled minds that touched his own. "Have you heard of it? Do you have a copy here?"

"Bob we were chosen because we write books, sculpt sculptures, create symphonies, xerazac xeazacoolgies, build cathedrals, tune signing neutron stars— you are class II. Your worldline just does something stupid. You are the ringside seat."

"But what about my book? The book that started all?" asked Bob.

"Soft typewriter, or you after computers? Spiral programming. Electron tunneling in the DNA, oh that was after the Disaster. The important book is in your cells, you're fulfilling something in your genes. Something placed there by an accident of history, and another of sexuality."

"No, I stole a book tonight."

They laughed again. "Bob, you are the punchline, "Neville said. "You want a book for you? A little leisure reading? I'll get you one by the beetles. It is a few chambers over."

Bob tried to walk, but just pulsed and jerked around spasmodically. Some crude instinct took over and he began to snail-slide in the vast hexagonal hall. Some of the creatures watched as he passed through the honeycomb.

"The humans, the more sentimental ones, are interested in you," said Neville.

"Why?" asked Bob.

"I'll let you read about it."

They traveled a long time. If this was such an advanced race they should have mastered airport people-mover technology. Bob asked, "Why books? Can't these guys do digital? "Bob knew there'd be some answer he couldn't understand, but just hoped that his questions at least showed him to be a clever idiot—like a zoo monkey who stares and nods and pretends to understand for smiles and contraband popcorn. Not like a zoo snail who doesn't even realize that his leaf and stick are fabrications. Something in him rumbled dully. "If they can swap minds, why not just swamp info the same way?"

"Their word for world is Library. This is their religion."

When they came to another chamber, which looked so much like the first it could have been the first. Neville's eye stalk scanned the volumes carefully. "I wonder what happens if you read about your deeds. "His claw chose one. Bob saw the title was in English.

"Is this some sort of magic, I can read other languages?"

"No, Bob. I've just been spoofing you, mate. When the Yithian that displaced my psyche died, I became a sort of honored guest. I was studying you Bob. This is one of my volumes. Even though I died five hundred years after you. You were my study, you and the Great Race. I was what you would call a physicist, but that's only a limitation of your vocabulary. You, Bob, are a particle. I look at particles. Now you take a look at the book. Oh dear, you have me rhyming."

The flying polyps carry a brane of their space-time. In their universe the weak force is negligible, and Carbon 14 is the stable isotope. They emit probability-waves — hence their lapses from visibility. My great-grandfather's dig had weakened a Yithian barrier in late 2012. By the sort of cosmic co-incidence that limits the Yithian control of lesser beings, a large extinction event on the Eastern seaboard of the United States.

Bob was able to ask "What?" in the dream or vision or whatever-the-fuck and finished his "does that have to do with me?" in the dank hotel room.

He was holding on to the poetry book with the same claw—er hand as Neville's tome. "I am not responsible for anything. I am not cosmically important. I am cracking the fuck up."

He would get out of here. He would drive home. He would go to the police and tell them he was bug-fuck crazy. The clock read 11:11.

He realized that he didn't know where to drive so he flipped a coin.

He turned on Rudolf the Red Nosed Reindeer and sped into the night. When his Uncle Robert had cracked up in Bob's teens, it had been the long nights of winter that got him. One of his conversations with Uncle Bob told him, "You know Santa Claus is really up there. Don't need no wings to fly. You know what you need? Luck."

It's all fucking great Uncle Robert was institutionalized for fears that Santa was really watching him, flying through winter nights whistling some cheap jingle. Angels We Have Heard On High/ Tell Us To Go Out And Buy, yeah, that's the shit.

Tonight was just crap. Bob had seen all the specials all the 2012 garbage. His uncle had been nuts. The job had been nuts. He could just hole up and get through the night. It was so damn dark here, he had wandered off main highways for sure. FOOD GAS ahead. Get a burger, get some orange juice for Christ's sake.

He pulled into a normal non-Twilight Zone station with cars and people and a big green BP gas sign and a McDonalds. He took the book with him. He ordered a Big Mac, large Diet Coke, and a cherry pie. It wasn't a value meal. Bob didn't order by number. He hoped that meant something. He sat on yellow and brown furniture looking at the deserted playscape. He ate his food, he read a last poem:

Tritina as Improved Bible

The human race began as a fart, I swear by my poesy and Art
Farted from Azathoth at the nine angled center
Consciousness and speech are the bubble

Rejoice oh might humans you do come from the center
And as inflating gas bags ours is a pretty bubble
Shiny with war and love, of course and Art

Raise your Yule mugs to the chaotic center,
As mindful of us as your dog is of human art
Philosophize that you are really not a bubble

Azathoth blows no more bubbles, the center does not hold
No more merriment in wine or love or Art.

What a cheerful little fuck. Merry Christmas to you Edward Pickman Derby. Bob walked over to the seven-foot-tall Frazier Fir that stood between the garbage

26

can and the napkin and utensil island. He admired the tiny multi-colored Charismas lights that blinked on and off, the ornaments from Wal-Mart, the little stockings with employees's names in red and green glitter. He said quietly, "I hate fucking cones. I hate fucking poetry. Merry fucking Christmas." He lay the copy of Edward Pickman Derby's Azathoth and Other Horrors among the fake red and green foil wrapped presents, and head out into the night.

Reg was outside. He was smoking a stolen cigarette. "Yo," he said, plainly. "It's done."

"What?"

"Like you said when you finally picked up the phone after all the calls, after all the messages I'd left—kill Frank. He was gonna cut us out, then hand us over to the cops or the mob. He admitted it and everything, like you said he would."

Christ, Bob thought. That was the flipside of his moment in that great jumble of a body. Something else had been in his. The difference between wearing your dirty underwear another day, and sliding into somebody else's for a day. Uncle Robert had said that too when Bob was a kid, about something, but Bob had forgotten what the analogy had been for. Blood surged up to Bob's face, feeding the brain, offering a sudden clarity. Every synapse blazed. Something stretched toward him from far away, from the deep space in his mind, from the long end of time in which Bob felt trapped like a rat in tar. It was spectacular, tentacular. Oh dear, Bob was rhyming. There was knowledge in that old library, in this new brain. He could use it.

"The body, where is it now?" Bob said. "Did you hide it, somehow?"

"Shelby Forest, like you said, man," Reg said, "with the truck. Then I hitched here to meet up like we talked about. Gas and go. What the hell, Bob "Reg took a step closer. "You said this was gonna all work out. You had a plan. You said we were gonna kick back and take it easy, that you knew a place to lay low far from here. Mexico, right? Passports and shit."

"Well, remember the next thing you have to do now, Reg?" Bob said. "To get the photo on the fake passport to match your face?" He smiled. "Remember. Take the gun, put it under your chin, like so?" Bob demonstrated with the stub of his cherry pie. Reg reached to the small of his back and pulled out his snub-nosed revolver. It went under chin, like so. His eyes were wide, scared like a deer in fire. Reg fired, jerked, collapsed, and his ass hit the ground before his skullcap did.

As Bob drove away, mouth full of whatever was really in cherry pies, the radio said something about Australia, but he didn't notice. He felt a charge. Something special he'd brought back with him from wherever, heh, no, whenever he thought, he'd been. Some deeper understanding. The universe was a billiard table, or at least that's how Bob imagined it. He'd met the men with the cues. He could do a trick shot of his own now too. Just did one, on Reg, to match the one his Yithian interloper had done on Frank. There was a certain symmetry, you know?

And the book. He could just imagine what would happen to the next curious guy to pick it up. Fuckin' Tennessee. Could be at Mickey D'sa week before anyone who can do more than sign his name with an X even checks it out, no fuckin' doubt. Bob missed the book, but knew he had to head away from it. Keep driving down that long dark road. Certainly don't turn back for it. Definitely don't end up driving down the wrong lane into someone's brights. Then, a canister tanker full of neurotoxin. Just before he plowed into it, Bob did see something red flying in the sky. It could have been Santa.

Don Webb was born on April 30, which accounts for his weirdness. Author of 16 books, he has stories in hundreds of venues, from Fantasy and Science Fiction *to* Interzone *to* Trucker's USA. *Don has over 40 stories in "best of year" lists and collections since 1986. His next fiction collection is a Wildside Double—A* Velvet of Vampyres *and Don's collected space opera,* The War with the Belatrin

Nick Mamatas is the author of several novels, including Sensation *and* Bullettime. *His short fiction has appeared in* New Haven Review, Asimov's Science Fiction *and in many other venues; and his Lovecraftian short fiction can be found in* Lovecraft Unbound, Future Lovecraft, New Cthulhu, *and* Black Wings II. *Nick's editorial work has been nominated for the Hugo, World, Fantasy, and Bram Stoker awards—his latest anthology is* The Future is Japanese, *co-edited with Masumi Washington.*

MAYOR NIMBLE MAKES IT KNOWN
STEVE AYLET[T]

I HAVE DECIDED THAT ALL TRADE WILL BE CONDUCTED BY THE EXCHANGE OF LARD. AND THEN I WILL TRANSFORM INTO A GIANT DRAGONFLY.

LARD? A DRAGONFLY? BUT SURELY THE PEOPLE WON'T STAND FOR IT.

PEOPLE HAVE S FIVE AT A LOLLING AM FLOWERS L A DIFFICU NIGHTMAR

THEM FEAST ON DIAGRAMS. YOU REMEMBER WHEN I SAID I WOULD GIVE BIRTH TO SOME SORT OF HEN?

AND ITS GIANT BEAK LIKE A LOCOMOTIVE'S SNOW PLOW WILL STAB YOU BADLY! A DISCOURAGING TRIUMPH AND THE STRANGE COLOR THIS MAKES ON THE MAPS OF HISTORY!

HORIZON HEN

KNOW THE HEN

THE HEN IS MY CONCERN

HEN YEAR, SURE, I REMEMBER.

CAME TO NOTHING. YET ENERGY EXPENDED RAN PERSONAL UNDERPANTS FURNACE FOR TWO WEEKS.

THAT FURNACE DOES NOTHING BUT BURN PERFECTLY GOOD UNDER- PANTS.

YOU UNDERSTAND, OLLY - PARTIALLY. YOUR CAREER OF UNOBTRUSIVE INEFFICIENCY IS CHEAPLY PLAUSIBLE AND FLIMSILY FORGIVEN. KUDOS.

T A HIGHER DUTY DANGLES INTO MY EYES. I AM NOW CONVERTING CONSEQUENCE INTO STEAM.

... IT'S THE ELEVATION OF LACK TO INDEBTEDNESS. MY TECHNIQUE IS TO PLUCK THE RIPE COBRA FROM THE SUMMER HEDGE. ALARM SETS A SOUL OFF BALANCE.

OFF BALANCE? WHAT'S THE USE OF THAT?

A CENTRED M DOESN'T COME WHEN SUMMONE WHY WOULD HE? HOW MIGHT YOU DESCRIBE THAT CHIN OF YOUR

AILABLE?

PRECISELY THE ANSWER I EXPECTED - FROM YOU, AND THE MASSES.

OBEDIENCE BUILT IN LAYERS WILL NOT BE FRAGILE.

I STILL DON'T THINK-

THEIR MINDS ARE CLUTTERED AND CRAMPED BY CELEBRITY'S HERALDRY. WE'VE NOTHING TO FEAR. ANNOUNCE IT TOMORROW, AND YOU WILL BE REWARDED.

THE MAYOR PLANS TO MORPH INTO A HUGE BUG. THIS IS INTENDED AS A SAFETY VALVE. THRIVE YOU ALL.

ELOQUENCE IN MINIATURE, OLLY. COME GET YOUR REWARD IN MY OFFICE NOW.

OH BOY! I SURE WILL!

SPANISH GOLD!

CHRONICLE

OLLY RESEMBLES AN EXHAUSTED CHIMP

EATS OWN LEGS FOR THE FUN OF IT

MOCKERY EXTINGUISHES HIS COMMAND, OBVIOUSLY

WHY AM I AN EXHAUSTED CHIMP?

ONLY YOU CAN ANSWER THAT ONE, OLLY. BUT YOUR RECTANGULAR STUPEFACTION IS QUAINT.

A BRITTLE HAMME NO HAMMER ATAL BUT IT MAY DISTR REMEMBER HE YEAR? WHEN CHALLENGED I UNVEILED A STRANGE PIG.

THAT PIG WAS DRESSED IN A PETTICOAT AND BONNET. IN A FLASH ALL PAST OMISSIONS RECEDED.

I STILL OWN THE SKELETON OF THAT CREATURE. I HAVE BEEN PAINTING IT WITH MODELLING ACRYLLICS. THE SOLVENT SMELL IS ... QUITE HEADY.

YOUR OUTRAGEOUS ANTICS THREATEN EVERYONE. GET IT NOW?

I GUESS MY JOB'S GOT A BUNCH MORE COMPLICATED.

T I'M A SIMPLE AN. WHAT THE ELL'S GOING ON? NEVER REALLY NDERSTOOD EN YEAR. DID REALLY DO OMETHING WRONG?

BUY TEN POUNDS OF LARD

GO TO THE STORE ON CHARM STREET.

PAYING WITH LARD!

WHEN WAS YO I DREAM GROW UP INTEREST AND FI

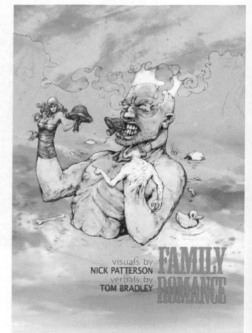

Function I

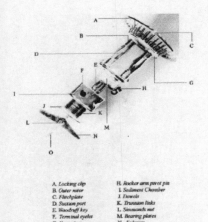

A. Locking clip	H. Rocker arm pivot pin
B. Outer rotor	I. Sediment Chamber
C. Flitchplate	J. Dowels
D. Suction port	K. Trunnion links
E. Woodruff key	L. Simmonds nut
F. Terminal eyelets	M. Bearing plates
G. Capacitor	N. Fulcrum
	O. Gudgeon pin

Function IV

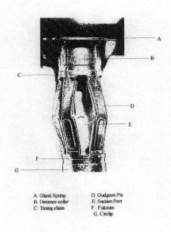

A. Gland Spring	D. Gudgeon Pin
B. Distance collar	E. Suction Port
C. Timing chain	F. Fulcrum
	G. Circlip

Function V

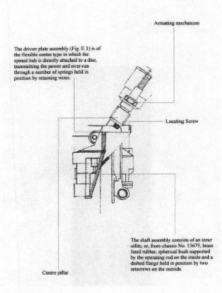

The driven plate assembly (Fig. E.1) is of the flexible centre type in which the splined hub is directly attached to a disc, transmitting the power and over-run through a number of springs held in position by retaining wires.

Actuating mechanism

Locating Screw

The shaft assembly consists of an inner oilite, or, from chassis No. 13675, brass lined rubber, spherical bush supported by the operating rod on the inside and a dished flange held in position by two setscrews on the outside.

Centre pillar

FUNCTION

Remote sound, a city's distant commotion;
the lonely hum of neon beams, a deserted
state fairground. Tenements, concrete turrets,
disconnect, thrown off the power grid.

There is no room or peace to sleep in this
darkness. The ghost-music of the nighttime shift,
a sonata composed of hydraulics,
the ram and pound, the daily skitter of tools

across factory floor, that lightning-thunder twist
of scrap metal threaded through the shredder feeds.
Lay your hand cards on the cracked pavement,
flick the switch. Imagine the machine stops.

Imagine the final product, turning the assembly-
line off. The gears slow. You forget
the march of pistons, the bluebottle racket
of striplighting. Silence. Stillness. Myth.

Adam Lowe & Chris Kelso

*Adam Lowe is a writer, publisher, live artist and producer from Leeds, UK. He
represented Yorkshire in The National Lottery's 12 Poets of 2012, for which he
was commissioned to write a poem for the Olympic Park. He has been an official
ambassador for the Cultural Olympiad since 2010 and has been writer-in-
residence at Zion Arts Centre, I Love West Leeds, Leeds Kirkgate Market and West
Yorkshire Playhouse. He has been commissioned by the Royal Exchange Theatre,
the BBC, Channel 4, Endemol and Freedom Studios, among others. His chapbook,*
Precocious, *was a reader nomination for the Guardian First Book Award. He is
currently working on a novel based on his acclaimed novella,* Troglodyte Rose,
*which was a finalist in the 2010 Lambda Literary Awards. He co-founded the
performance and literature development organisation DLS Enterprises and runs
Dog Horn Publishing. Find out more about him at* adam-lowe.com.

DANCE RECITALS
Lydia Fascia

Technicolor Prostitots Live at Radio City Music Hall

I cannot be the first bitch to notice the absolute fucking sickness of children's dance recitals. I'm required to attend two or three little girls' performances every year—It's meaningful to the girls that I'm there as I'm a dancer myself, and they want me to see their work. It hurts. It really does. In life, we all must make sacrifices. I would happily eat a condiment sandwich while washing my clothes in the bathtub with dish soap then walking 6 miles to therapy in exchange for a get out of jail free card. I would street canvass for Planned Parenthood in Salt Lake City. I'd dance naked for no money at all.

Having been an on-and-off-again "erotic dancer" for the past several years, I feel that I have developed a very special relationship with sexual exploitation. And holy fuck, do these "performances" reek of sexual exploitation. I've said many times that, were I a pedophile, I would look forward to recital season in the same way that the queers in NYC look forward to the Coney Island Mermaid Parade. These kids are painted up like the spawn of Jon Benet Ramsey and Rupaul. They wear enormous shiny earrings, and every. Single. Costume. Is so short that they wear some bullshit underwear over their actual underwear so that it doesn't "count" as being inappropriate. They're called "lollipops." What does one do with a lollipop? Suck on it. Sequins, lame, and gauzy lingerie passes for a costume, and the young ladies who don these "costumes" have no concept yet of provocation. They're doing what they've been instructed to do in terms of following the "visions" of their piece of shit teachers with BAs in dance from some piece of shit state school.

The program is usually sprinkled with a handful of extraordinarily age-inappropriate and culturally insensitive pieces. Their jackass teachers put them in revealing, fucked up, racist costumes. Most recently I saw a dance that was choreographed to the Pussycat Dolls song 'Jai Ho', in which the dancers wore Indian belly dance mock-ups, integrating their shitty modern dance technique and bollywood-esque imitations. There was a sheer flesh-toned meshing covering the parts of their bellies, where, as with the "special panties," to somehow make them less naked and therefore perfectly appropriate. I sat in the audience with my fuck-me-I'm-beautiful biracial cousin who is a classically trained ballet dancer. I saw the absolute indignation, disgust and confusion painted all over her perfect, perfect face. I honest to goodness covered my mouth to keep from laughing, and when the urge to burst out became too strong, it was all I could do to turn it into a sneeze or a cough.

The practice of stripping has, in the past, been referred to as "exotic dancing." As a community in which, believe it or not, some of us are actually aware of what's fucked up, exotic dancing is a perfect example. When erotic dancing first became popular nearly a century ago, white women wishing to whore it up on stage dressed as members of a different race or culture. Of course, a white woman onstage would be completely devastating. Men would be reminded of their daughters! Their nieces! Their sweet, young granddaughters! With this in mind, these women would make up their faces to look vaguely and generally Asian. They would perform some weird shit that was intended to look "exotic." Island women would also pop up everywhere from time to time. Everyone loves a hula girl.

My first question, which I formulated about ten years ago during one of my own dance recitals, is why the fuck do these mothers allow their children to walk around like painted fucking whores? These soccer moms, with their SUVs, their part-time jobs doing secretarial work for their husbands' independent plumbing businesses. These women, who care nothing about the world outside of their suburbs. These women who judge the little sluts at their daughters' middle schools, who meet up and go to coffee so that they can talk shit about the other moms who aren't present. These moms who don't let their thirteen-year olds kiss boys or dance with them at their stupid fucking school balls. These women. Why are these costumes okay to them? Because it's onstage, so it's "not real?" Because it's some tradition in the small-local-shitty-dance culture? Apparently, one mom, one Dr. Wendy Walsh got a clue based on a post on momlogic. com writing,

> Sexualizing children to this degree can only hurt all children everywhere. If this is the new benchmark for competitions, what are we teaching our baby girls who are just out of diapers? That their value lies in how well they can tempt and engage in sexual provocation?
>
> And I gotta ask: What are we dangling in the faces of men, whose natural responses to visual cues can so easily be triggered? With suggestive material like this available worldwide, it's no wonder that the proliferation of the child sex-slave trade continues.

Seriously, now. If these little cunts-in-training are receiving said training, how are they ever going to develop a sense of themselves as independent bitches who don't take no mess? Honestly. They're being conditioned to shake their shit and look sweet from the time they can walk. It's kind of a big deal. Feminist propaganda aside, little girls need room to breathe. Little girls need their early days—their childhoods—to figure out their shit. They don't need to be made to look like identical little baby Stepford shits, sculpted by the mold of their fucktard mothers, who are probably trying their best to make sure that their kids are leading enriching childhoods, but are failing horribly.

Now. The very last thing that I am is a prude. When it comes to matters of sexual expression, I don't give a fuck what consenting adults want to do with their bodies. Prostitution? Awesome. Be safe. Stripping? I've been there plenty. Just try to enjoy yourself. Fetish? Whatever floats your boat. Porn? Fuck yah. You're more adventurous than even I. But for the love of tits, these are kids! They don't realize or understand that they're being groomed to look like mini-pros!

Now. Here is where the stripping discussion comes into the picture. Erotic dancers paint their faces and turn their bodies into lies. They obviously dance either almost-naked or fully nude depending on which state or country where they work. They might be friends with one another, but when it comes to matters of performance, it becomes an insane competition where everyone is out for blood. It's the nature of the beast. Guys get their rocks off while the painted ladies shimmy and shake. Parents and family members have their junk stroked watching their kids make horrible mini-monsters of themselves. That, I don't understand. What is it about this demented, demoralizing practice of pageantry, perpetrated by teachers and parents, performed by tiny tots who know not what they do, that offers any merit? The world may never know.

It has been said that Miss Ginger is "this ultimate femme fatale. She's got this red hair and always-red lips and she just looks like she'll crush your skull after she fucks the shit out of you." She was once told that she "wasn't whitey-white! [She's] crazy out of [her] fucking mind! [She] transcends race! [She] defies gender [She's] like a tranny!" Finally, in a rare moment of sincerity, one of the world's greatest dickholes shared the following, "Miss Ginger, you're probably crazy. But you're a pretty nice lady, and I like hanging out with you." Miss Ginger is a crazed cunt-rag, but at least she's not an asshole. And she couldn't have said any of it better herself.

Wiggly Fetus - Alan M. Clark

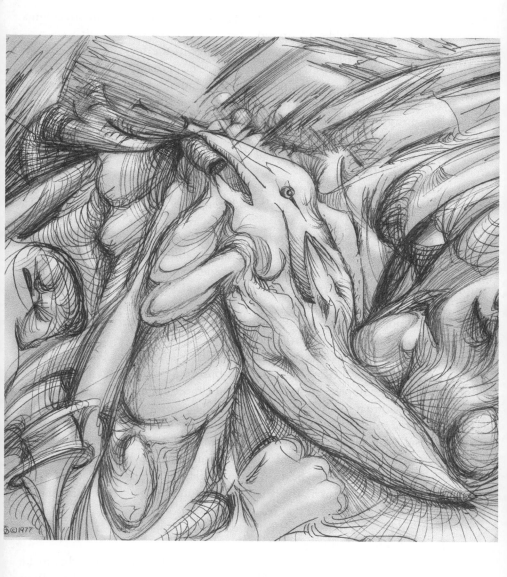

THE WETLANDS ARE BURNING
Nikki Guerlain

Slinking down a street on a cold wet night. The moon's gone black, the streetlights out. Scattered embers smolder all around.

Gazing out into the desolate street, I listen to the hiss of rain falling all around me. The gentle raindrops hit fire and make steam that lifts me up and urges me on. It all urges me on, now. I slip into the rain, knife in hand.

In the embers' pervasive, shifting glow, I catch the ghostly flicker of my sister Stella:Legs spread wide, back against wall, day-of-the-week panties on. Monday. Always the Monday underwear on.

I pause. I stop. Clench my tool of desire. I slide over to where my sister is, knowing that she'll be gone.

Scraping my tongue against an empty wall, I continue on. Unable to control the cutting desire to hold my sister in a bloody embrace, I hunt the streets to find a gash and a malleable face.

The taunts of my sister echo in my heartbeats: Get the Sugar Get the Sugar.

High-heel clicks penetrate the gloom. An unstable form appears, darker than the embers, the asphalt, the night, the storm. I quiet my own heels, to steal her with surprise. Raising my hopes, raising me higher. My knife grows heavy with swelling desire.

She stumbles, just then, looks behind her and catches herself. I slide along the wall, seemingly unnoticed. But I notice.

I notice that her dress fits tightly, and that she wears no coat. Ambling down the road, she snuffles and cries. Broken heart, broken home, broken girl all alone, blitzed, consumed, completely unaware that I'm almost upon her.

I clear my throat to let her know I'm there. She stops, apparently frozen with fear. I spin her around.

She lets out a scream, and I set her throat free with a flick of my hand. The dying in my arms is a horrible sound. Hope sprouts wings and flies from her eyes, the fall of rain muffling the wingbeats. A veil of Stella falls over her face as she swans to the ground in a graceful arch. The flames flare around her hips, beckoning me in, the voice of my sister telling me that it's been too long

What's this mean, Dirty Little Machine?

The wetlands are burning.

I hear no voices but the echo of my thoughts, barking mad dogs that make me feel like a small child slapped across the room. Blood smells like cherry pie. Rain feels black. Red screams.

I tell myself over and over that only live things swim upstream. I take the bar of soapfrom between my teeth and crawl to the kitchen for something shiny to cut with, knowing that by the time I get there I won't feel like hurting myself.

I'm licking the juice of a blood orange as it drips down the knife in my hand. I'm feeling the hotm calm air turn to a stir, rustling the curtains. A storm's coming, and I can already feel the sludge of dark mud ripping through landscape, spilling into sky, bleeding black down. Unearthed bodies, bones and stone standing upright though swayed to the side.

> What's this all mean, Dirty Little Machine?
> Keep your hands to yourself, I say.
> Get the sugar. Get the sugar. Get the sugar
> But I need the sugar.

Dark against a sky of fire, trees sway like maple syrup. Hair wet against my skin, her bones sharp against mine, I tell her that I love her. But her eyes, a gravestone grey obscured by fog, drift away from mine, and her features melt into something not Stella.

"I love you, too, "she says. But her lips don't move, and her words sink, then quickly fade away like the dead chink of driftwood wind-chimes in a lazy breeze. I let her body slide off mine, to crumple at the base of the giant electrical pylon where Eyeless Chucky has a makeshift nest. Her voice floats, waivers inside my skull: Chucky is coming.

I hear his cart's jangly metal squeal, and the barking mad legion of extra meaty three-legged dogs that pull it like some bastardized Iditarod in Hell. I crouch behind a large chunk of slate obscured by sea grass the color of autumn leaves and fire, smelling of smoke and char.

The dogs easily maneuver the twisted and uneven path through the sand dunes, moving like a thick fluid through a crevasse, as if one. Chucky whips the dogs mercilessly, a round creature dressed head to toe in black. He smells of rotten meat and old cum, of things not so much gone bad but never good. Of carrion and burned live things.

My mouth tastes of vomit. There is no getting used to his smell, or the feeling of hopelessness that makes my eyes feel like they've dropped into my lungs when I breathe.

What's this mean, Dirty Little Machine?

It means that no matter how much I fuck you and kill you, you won't let me be.

Get the Sugar. Get the Sugar. Get the Sugar.

And there she is. Again. Relentless. Flickering in and out, her back against a rock, smelling all pink like cotton candy, legs spread open wide, Monday underwear, wet. She's stroking her naked belly with one hand, while her other strokes a small breast. Her hand trails from her belly to her wet, cotton covered slit.

C'mon, Lou get the Sugar

But her lips don't move. They haven't for over twenty years. I'm sorry. I'm sorry. I say over and over and sweat. I'm sorry. No. No. No. I shake my head. Not again. But my body betrays me and my pants grow heavy and strain.

I will myself to look away from her. To look back to Chucky and his mad dogs and the body— the Stella But Not. Another Stella But Not to join the others, disfigured beasts.

At some point, Chucky had stripped off his clothes and sent the dogs off whining. Now his naked body stands over the Stella But Not. His body is riddled with scars, and a thick length of splintered wood stands in the place where his left leg should be.

His face is a boiling pot of oatmeal with a dark purplish starfish-like swirl of a scar where his eyes ought to go. His sparse, moldy hair hangs limp and long and heavy from grease. With his thick, dirty hand he pumps away at the fat, angry meat between his thighs. Stream after stream of spermatozoa the size of tadpoles hit the mangled Stella But Not and burrow into her skin, molding and shaping it, growing it into fur.

The Stella But Not begins to growl as hand turns to paw. I look away when Chucky goes into his nest to grab his ax. I always have to look away when the dogs start screaming, and there's that giant yelp of a newborn piercing through all the madness then the grunting and panting of Chucky as he takes his whelp from behind.

And always, always, there she is, haunting me and pushing me on, working her fingers in and out of her gash, dead ghost eyes upon mine, lips never moving but always promising, relentless.

What does this mean, Dirty Little Machine?

Get the Sugar. Get the Sugar. Get the Sugar.

Nikki Guerlain lives in Portlandia Suburbia. Her work appears both online and in print. Various bits of information and links to her work can be found at nikkiguerlain. com.

Many Madonnas - Alan M. Clark

MAGIC VERSUS MYSTICISM
Don Webb

Recently I visited the "Metaphysical" section of a bookstore. As a writer of occult books, I usually find this the least interesting section—most of the books are a sort of low grade pornography promising unlimited powers or describing how non-existent threats may be avoided. I prefer fiction, anthropology and the philosophy sections. I was looking over the titles, which ranged from some fairly scholarly books on Tantra to *Channelings from Lemuria*, when the loud whispers of a young couple behind me caught my attention. They were debating spending their hard earned cash on either of two books. To avoid being contentious I will make the titles—*Tuning into Universal Bliss* and *Practical Sorcery*. The heated discussion ended with "Look it doesn't matter anyway, all this crap is the same." I didn't wait around to see which volume of crap was selected. I saw a friend of mine in the adjoining coffee shop and I left to pursue my caffeine addiction.

I realized that the sentiment expressed in the argument is widely held—it is perhaps even a mainstay of the occult industry. But there is a fundamental difference between mysticism and magic and one's choice of paths reflect what kind of a person you are, and what you desire to become. Both techniques use bliss as either as means or goals, both give the users a connection to aspects of reality that the average human does not have (or want). Both are not supported by our host culture, and seem either quaint or at their most sinister—examples of a flight from reason. I would like to discuss the differences, but before I start I should say I am practitioner of the magical path and I am not pretending to be impartial.

Human beings have an innate gift for moments of transcendence. Some people theorize this is due to quantum states of the brain; some people call the phenomena having a soul, other simply assert that is an ultimate mystery that cannot be explained. Transcendence has certain characteristics—it annihilates the day-to-day sense of self. It imbues every object and perception with meaning. It gives a sense of vastness, calmness —even bliss. Various drug users from William James to Timothy Leary have caused this state, others reach it through yoga, dance, chanting, or even looking at shiny surfaces. What separates the magician from the mystic is the follow up state. When transcendence ends, depression sets in. One no longer sees God, or is God—the rivers of meaning that can flow from various mundane objects or activities cease to flow, and all the yet-to-be done deeds of daily life remain yet to be done. But what did the experience mean?

For the mystic transcendence points to a realm of perception that over-shadows the day-to-day world. It is Heaven, or the Realm of Forms, or Haqiqah.

46

Regaining the moment of transcendence is paramount. Since withdrawal from the senses is a viable method, mankind developed monasteries and hermitages. Or if methods of excitation are used—like dance, religious frameworks supporting the dance or the festival came into being. The mystic is drawn to philosophies that see day-to-day life as meaningless. The connections to this world must philosophically be shatteredso that greater periods of transcendence can be entered into. Mysticism, although it may preach holism, is ultimately about separation.

The magician reflects on transcendence as a time of power. Unlike her mystic brother, she does not see herself as the unworthy receiver of a gift from beyond. Rather she senses transcendence as a time of perceiving and therefore acting in underdeveloped or hidden aspects of herself. Since she sees her heightened state as part of her own being, she reasons that the state must exist for the betterment of her own being. Since the transcendent state is seen as part of the self, the self is seen as vast. Furthering all aspects of the self—economic, spiritual, artistic, etc. becomes as important a goal for the magician, as curtailing all aspects of the self are for the mystic. For the magician transcendent sates are a foretaste of the Future; for the mystic transcendent states are an experience of Otherness. The ultimate image of a mystic would be the cartoon angel plucking his harp in praise of something vaster than himself; for the magician the ultimate image is Becoming a god or goddess. The occult book community sells its books, cards, tape sets to both groups—and has a strong interest in neither group being very aware of its goals, which would lead to certain independence beyond consumerism.

Two traditions reflect the magical path par excellence one arouse in Egypt and took shape in response to Christian thinking/repression. The other arose on the Indian subcontinent and took form in response to Mogul thinking/repression. Both began when traditional temple practices were outlawed, and so human had to do it all in their heads. When worship was no longer a sacrificial exchange in a physical temple, it moved into the realm of the Mind—and hence either into mysticism or magic. In Egypt the magical path became known as Hermeticism. In India it became the Vama Marg or Left Hand Path. Both groups were occasionally covered over by the ice of monotheism, but both traditions remain and are being remanifested in the West as a synthesis of the two—called the Left Hand Path. I have trod the Left Hand Path for most of my life. I have done so in a formal setting (in the Temple of Set) since 1989. Because of the strong influence the Hermetic path has had on English magic, I will focus on it more in this article,

The Egyptians early on discovered and idealized the practice of magic. The famous French Egyptologist Étienne Drioton (1881-1961) traced the roots of the Hermetic Tradition to a spell in *The Book of Felling Apep*, "Khepra Kheper Kheperu"—"The Self evolving god evolved himself and his cosmos." The nature

47

of the magician's path is laid bare. The magician, by entering a transcendent state gets a glimpse of her unmanifested self. Intrigued and empowered by this vision she seeks to change her day-to-day life so that she becomes more resonant with this state. This means she seeks to control more and more of her life. Notice this is not a top-down control or rigidity of life, but a fluid life space where evolution is possible. As she controls more and more of her life—more aspects of her life bear her stamp. In short she creates more currents, objects and situations in her life. She evolves herself and by so doing, evolves the world. By living in a world that is more and more her self-creation she creates a world that matches the powerful feelings she has in her moments of transcendence. Of course while this practical life-work has been going on, she has learned better techniques of the will that lead to longer, stronger more focused transcendent states. The Egyptian concept of self-creation was never a central religious theme until the ending of Egyptian paganism. The Romans cut off the economic feed to the temples in the third century; the newly popular religion Christianity suppressed them. The two inevitable groups emerged—the world-hating Gnostics and the world-affirming Hermeticists. Both flourished in Late Antiquity, both were suppressed—and their writings nearly lost.

In 1460 the writings of the Corpus Hermetica found their way to Europe. They proclaimed a religion of the mind, and their effect on the Renaissance and the Reformation were so great that Lutheran Bishop James Heiser recently evaluated the writings of Marsilio Ficino and Giovanni Pico della Mirandola as an attempted "Hermetic Reformation." (Heiser, James D., Prisci Theologi and the Hermetic Reformation in the Fifteenth Century, Repristination Press: Texas, 2011). The texts were attributed to Hermes Trismegistus and described a positive universe where knowledge was the key to power and pleasure. Notions that create the modern world from belief in progress, science, and public education came from this encounter. The effect of these texts on the magical lore of Europe cannot be overstated. The French occultist Eliphas Levi said of one of the documents in the Corpus, the Emerald Tablet, that it "contains all magic in a single page." Most magical societies in Europe and the Americas see the texts as a map to greater consciousness—the Rosicrucians, the OTO, the Hermetic Brotherhood Luxor, the Hermetic Brotherhood of the Golden Dawn, Fraternitas Saturni, and the Stella Matuntia are but a few examples. Albert Pike, founder of modern Freemasonry, writes extensively about Hermes Trismegistus as a mythical founder of Masonry.

The Hermetic path begins withdrawing one senses and attention from the Objective Universe and sending this attention and intent into the Subjective Universe. This leads to actual experience of self-deification. Consider the following lines from Book XI, where the Mind explains to Hermes that imagination is the key to power—contrast this idea with the God-centered, text-centered worldview of the middle ages. Reading these lines one can almost feel the coming into being of the Renaissance:

Command your soul to go anywhere, and it will be there quicker than your command. Bid it go to the ocean and again it is there at once . . . Order it to fly up to heaven and it will need no wings . . . and if you wish to break through all this and to contemplate what is beyond, it is in your power. If you do not make yourself equal to God you cannot understand him. Like is understood by like. Grow to immeasurable size. Be free from every body, transcend all time. Become eternity and thus you will understand God. Suppose nothing to be impossible for yourself. Consider yourself immortal and able to understands everything: all ages, sciences, and the nature of every living treasure.

These texts had lain in a Macedonian monastery waiting for their moment to rewrite the cultural paradigm of Europe, to foster in a Faustian Age. Yet the Corpus is not a magician's handbook. It is a philosophical treaty to aid the prepared mind to experience self-deification. But one does not leap from getting home from the marketplace to such exercises in Will. Such things may be simulated intellectually, but for the formula of self-deification to work, the seeker needs to experience power in her circumstances that shows she has an influence beyond the laws of the mechanical universe. The training in philosophy goes hand in hand with training in magic—the art of achieving goals beyond what might be ordinarily expected by changing one's subjective universe. The books for training these things were (as the historical sections of this book will show) systemically destroyed by monotheists, who must first and foremost take a stand against the religion of the mind. However, the lore of Egypt does fight back.

In the early nineteenth century an Armenian Giovanni Anastasi (note the Greek roots of his name ανάστασις = "Resurrection") began using his position as Swedish-Norwegian consul in Egypt to sell large quantities of papyri and other antiquities to various European museums. Among these were the first examples of what came to be called the "Greek Magical Papyri." These were a treasure trove of Egyptian magic written in the most part by professional translators in Greek and Roman Egypt. Here were the lower rungs of the ladder that lead to the heights of the Corpus. Egypt had long been ruled by Temple-based magical practice. As imperial Rome began to see the established clergy as a threat, Romans removed their tax base, and later Copts simply closed and desecrated them. The practice of religion and magic stopped being based on material culture, and by necessity became a religion of the mind. This is an exact historical parallel to Indian Tantrics' resistance to Mogul rulers. The Temple-based practice became a self-based practice and quite naturally became a religion of the mind—called in Sanskrit the Vama Marg, or Left Hand Path.

49

The Hermetic path was one of revolt from the world, but not denial of it. Unlike their compatriots the Gnostics—Hermetics did not see the world as bad or deficient. Like their Left Hand Path brethren they saw pleasure as a worthwhile goal—and the key to a good life was mixing the bliss of the mind (gnosis) with skills in the world (episteme). This is the same synthesis that has remanifested in modern Left Hand Path groups. Their struggles to use the Will as a focus to obtain the fullness of the Mind, and to use the fulfillment of Desire as a lesson to the soul of its godlike potential is our struggle.

Various deities are often invoked in the Greek Magical Papyri—the figure of Hermes being the most common. But surprisingly a figure that had been unpopular in Egyptian religion for centuries makes a new stand. Set, the demonic initiator of Osiris, returns in his oldest role—the Ur-Heka or Senior Magician. For the Hermetic seeker this figure, who rebels against cosmic injustice—who loves darkness and mystery—who gives us the meteoric iron to making birthing knives—returns as ruler of the world. The magician does not appeal to Set, but Becomes Him. He boasts of his power over Osiris— "I am the Griffith of the West, who holds Osiris in my paws." The god of stasis is slain. The magicians of Late Antiquity faced a time when older paradigms were being eroded and this lead to seeking newer paradigms in the more ancient world. Set, culture of Naquada, who had facilitated the very coming into being of civilization was again needed as a friend of mankind. Not as provider, but as a life model for some at least. The old watchword of the HermeticistKhepher is alive and well in the world as Xeper, the watchword of the Temple of set.

Choose well your glimpse of the world beyond—is it a reason to renounce this world, or to become the god of your own?

Actually I did see the young couple leave with *Practical Sorcery* in their unwashed but brave hands. Perhaps I will see them again.

For bio see page 30.

Penmanship - David Aronson

PENMANSHIP CLASS:

(an examination of Japanese language pedagogy
in the Intermountain region of the United States
during the climactic years of the Nixon administration)

Tom Bradley

The pen is the tongue of the brain.
—Miguel Cervantes

Before Dai Nippon's main island was turned into a nuclear no-go zone, it would sometimes feel the sole of my foot. I'd ride the ferry boat from the figurative leper isolation colony that constitutes my secret place of banishment, and visit my old friend, Fukuoka-sensei.

He was remotely antique and elegant. The latter quality has always taken an emetic effect on my stomach lining; but Fukuoka-sensei managed it well, in his indigo robes and satin slippers that whistled along the rice straw mats in his tiny, mostly paper home.

His English was impeccable. At first I assumed it must have been gotten purely through books, as is the case with so many venerable gentlemen of the Extreme Orient. But occasionally tinctures of American idioms would seep in, substandard usages and even the odd vulgarism, all belonging to a certain region, and a specific epoch, with which I happen to be familiar. So I asked him if he'd been there.

He averted his eyes and replied, "I'd rather not speak about that."

It took me many ferry boat rides, over the course of an entire year, to get him to allow that he'd been there. "All right, yes," he sighed. "Forty years ago I was foolish enough to try teaching at a private college preparatory institution. It was a hell-hole deep in the Mormon Mecca."

As far as that prep school can be reconstructed from Fukuoka-sensei's reluctant reminiscences, it seems to have been the only place in the Intermountain Region pretentious enough, in those pre-"economic miracle" days, to offer classes in Nihongo. The board members were too rich and powerful to trouble themselves with the small matter of faculty accreditation.

And it was there that "Mr. Fukuoka" (as he became known in context) encountered the graphological phenomenon called Biffy Wamsutter.

The Wamsutter brat's ideograms lost their barbarian squareness halfway through the first lesson. Fukuoka-sensei told me he'd never seen anything like it. The horrible boy's precocious virtuosity extended with equal ease from ink and brush to ballpoint, to chalk, to Ticonderoga two-point-five—any medium, in fact, including spraypaint on brick walls (his favorite). He could imitate the vastly divergent styles of Mao and Zhou Enlai, and almost anybody else, except the great Japanese

52

calligraphers, at whom he wouldn't deign to glance. And he boasted about doing all of his homework and much of his classwork on "heroic doses" of mescaline and psilocybin.

"No problem," Biffy would say, and strut his noodle-thin two meters in front of the blackboard. Bluish eyeballs swimming under dope-swollen lids, he would talk in ways belying his degenerate appearance. "It's not as though you have to achieve chiaroscuro or perspective or anything like that. This is a non-art, contrived for no other reason than to flatter the mediocrity Confucianism thrives on. It's two-dimensional and decorative, like interior design: the kind of thing that gives fags tiny brittle boners."

A whole sentence of Biffy's characters could look like a rout of Hieronymous Bosch's orgiasts cavorting without joy on the lip of some narcotized Gehenna, a disproportionate number of them losing a forearm to the ravenous anal jaws of their androgynous partner. He could turn every new kanji into something that elicited wicked snickers and cries of "Asemic, ma-a-a-an!" from the other youngsters. With equal ease, he coaxed moans of stunned enchantment from both sides of the teacher's podium. With his left hand this cruel bully-boy could dash off a character that possessed more virtu than all the labored-over scribbles ever wrought at midnight by his lonesome teacher. And Mr. Fukuoka had to fight a life-death struggle with murderous envy, every fourth period.

"I intend to read Lu Xun and the other red-hot mainlanders," Biffy puffed one afternoon, the salty Utah sun blasting off his unbrushed orthodontia. "Who have the Nips to offer? Yukio Mishima?"

And, of course, by that late date, all it took was the bare mention of the beautiful writer's name to bring down the house, as it were. Demolished, for the remainder of the period, was any vestige of the Asian-style teacher-veneration that Mr. Fukuoka had tried to establish, in his fervid desire to saturate the children in Yamato culture.

Biffy incited the sluttier cigarette-husky girls and the more gorgeous boys to dub Mr. Fukuoka "Yucky Mishy-mash," and to snuggle up to him in the lunch hall, tickling, whispering and insinuating a physical resemblance between their Japanese teacher and that brilliant fascist novelist.

"Whence derives the uncanny, malignant telepathy of Caucasoid youth?" Fukuoka-sensei asked me one day as we knelt at his low lacquerware table, sipping unfermented tea from thimble-sized earthenware. "Have they emotional X-ray machines built into their blond heads? They're the best argument in favor of the existence of Romish Lucifer's legions that I've ever encountered in my life."

Though I was once a "Caucasoid youth" myself, I was no less mystified than my honorable host. How could the kids have known that their teacher sometimes secretly blushed in restroom mirrors and shop windows, and quietly flattered himself that he looked, from behind at least, a bit like a shorter version of that famous Nihonjin?

When the news of Yukio Mishima's death reached the eyes and ears of teenaged Salt Lake City (a couple of years late, of course, tardy as the moribund Maoist myth), the Wamsutter monster used it to torment and test Mr. Fukuoka even further. He began bringing blown-up xeroxes of the mad genius' narcissistic photos of himself in nothing but a loincloth, and parading them around the room.

In extreme old age, my sad friend was nothing like what the little sociopaths would've called a "swisher." And I assume his mannerisms hadn't been much broader four decades earlier. But still, with all the pernicious clairvoyance of godless adolescence, his students were able to surmise the nature of certain personal proclivities with which, he assured me, he had "never asked to be born." And, though among their own ranks they counted a disproportionate number of children who shared, both latently and blatantly, those same tendencies, they still sizzled with glee each time Biffy's flaunted Mishima photos succeeded in nailing their "teachie-poo-sensei" behind his desk with involuntary penile erections. His charges took advantage of his paralysis to run amok.

I was told, with a shudder, about the time Biffy smuggled in an issue of the National Geographic that featured a breathtaking pictorial on the Haddaka Matsuuri in Okayama. There were splendid full-page, strobe-lit shots of three thousand gleaming young men in nothing but loincloths, purifying themselves by pouring cold water on each other, and scrambling through the Saidaji Temple, under the anonymity of midnight darkness, to gain possession of a pair of holy amulets.

"I guess the cold water is to prevent things from getting really out of hand, huh, Sensei?" taunted Biffy, rubbing his forearm from wrist to elbow. "I mean, a law-abiding country like Japan can't permit its young men to have bloody orgies and cannibal holocausts, right? At least not on Japanese soil. We can't have the youth engaging in public displays of" (shifting into a camp lisp) "fisticuffs."

As always, that word brought the whole class, even the nice virginal prepubescent boys, to their knees with laughter. Other flippant voices joined in, cracking with sadistic delight and hormonal upheaval. The students did not forget to raise their pale hands first, as though classroom deportment hadn't already been pulverized.

"Howcome only dorks and frat-rats do stuff like this in America?"

"Do you think the Saidaji monks could recruit even thirty guys, let alone three thousand, if somebody put the word out that girls were interesting people, too?"

"Mr. Fukuoka? Why do you suppose this kind of festival is necessary only in countries where everybody's so polite?"

"Sensei, exactly what shape and size are these two amulets?"

54

"Oooh, yes, I do indeed love a good amulet!"

"Teachie-poo!" squawked the Wamsutter brat, "I believe I've experienthed an awakening of thorts! "He stuck out his elongated buttocks and duck-waddled among the desks, actually breaking wind in the faces of the females—

"—who seemed to love it!" marveled my friend, still appalled after all these decades. There was the tiniest suspicion of tears in the corners of his long eyes.

Mr. Fukuoka pleaded to be transferred to proctor sophomore home-room instead of junior. And he was promised that next year, by which time it would be too late, he could. But there was no "switching horse's-asses in midstream," which was the Latter-Day-Saintly way of saying that nobody else wanted, every morning of his or her working life, to face the fatal combination of Biffy and an appreciative audience of splinter-Mormon boarding students from the uncivilized southern desert.

The vicious goon daily took pains to make it clear that, since there was nary a Mandarin teacher in all the Intermountain West in those days of the Cultural Revolution, it was only by default that he'd enrolled himself in Japanese class (and, along with him, unfortunately, his retinue of Satanic lieutenants, the pagan polygamist spawn). Biffy was there, he emphasized through word and gesture, for no other reason than to learn the "alphabet of Chairman Mao" —who, of course, by that time had already lost at least ninety-five percent of his cachet among adult intelligentsia.

Mr. Fukuoka had been forced, at the hands of this miraculously talented pituitary case, to suffer the worst consequences of a sexuality which, at that time and place, was deemed abominable. By a sheer self-abnegating act of pious will, by "going cold turkey," as the dope-addicted students would solemnly put it, Mr. Fukuoka had sacrificed the health of his atrophying prostate gland, the better to concentrate on the pursuit of his vocation, to spend his nights alone grading piles of student kanji exercises. And sometimes he nurtured his ardent, isolated soul, in spite of the mortification it brought to his heart, by masturbating all over Biffy's themes—

"—so beautiful that it was necessary to hold them in front of a candle to make sure they were composed of mere markings on paper!"

It was impossible to shake off the agonizing awareness of the vast loss to the world that the Wamsutter boy's tragic strain of self-destructiveness entailed. Meanwhile, the lad himself bothered with neither the kana nor the conversation units, and he made vulgar restroom sounds with his lips during dictation and language lab exercises. So Fukuoka-sensei felt academically justified in taking what he considered a drastic measure: he called a parent-teacher conference.

Filling my cup, my old friend looked me in the eye (an unaccustomed behavior on these islands), and murmured, "Perhaps, being from Utah yourself, you won't find it surprising to hear that my bold pedagogical maneuver disconcerted

55

neither the boy nor his horrendous m-m-m—" He gagged on the M-word.

As regards the latter personage, Fukuoka-sensei had special words, which he punctuated with a gradual crescendo of fists on the fragile table. "Grendel's dam," he began, "with grisly grasp monster of women, who unleashed this kin of Cain upon the earth—if I may paraphrase the national epic of the accursed race that bred this monstrosity."

"My race, too, Sensei."

But that meek interjection went unheard, as my honorable host gnashed his linguistic fangs deeper into the throat of Biffy's sick nightmare of a female parent. As it turns out, this "dried-up furui gaikokujin baishun" showed up at the conference only to announce, "My sweetie-pie can mail-order whatever diplomas he wants from the back pages of Hustler."

Calligraphy ink and midori-cha splashed around my head in black and chartreuse arcs. Fukuoka-sensei began smashing the ink sticks that I was supposed to be grinding. He snatched a rare marten-hair calligraphy brush from behind my ear and sent it like a pub dart through the rice paper panel behind me. The more unbookish locutions of seventies America came to the fore, and Fukuoka-sensei began to display, in spurts and flashes, a near-native grasp of my own boyhood's idiom. This was surprising in a man who'd only managed to stomach my homeland for a single academic year.

"I tell you, it was a delicious privilege to flat-out-flunk this Biffy, this gross buffalo with gifted fingers instead of manure-caked hooves, this—"

He fell suddenly silent. His face became the lacquered mask of inscrutability that can be observed but not understood in every zone of this multiply nuked hell. He looked at me (or, rather, didn't) as if I were some outlandish species, barely discernible on the opposite shore of an ocean whose vastness he disdained to navigate. Henceforth Fukuoka-sensei would get whatever words of mine he wanted from books.

And this was the point in our penmanship classes when I usually decided it was time to board the ferry and return to the leper isolation colony.

Tom Bradley's latest books are Family Romance *(Jaded Ibis Press, illustrated by Nick Patterson),* A Pleasure Jaunt With One of the Sex Workers Who Don't Exist in the People's Republic of China *(Neopoiesis Press),* Even the Dog Won't Touch Me *(Ahadada Press),* Hemorrhaging Slave of an Obese Eunuch *(Dog Horn Publishing) and* Put It Down in a Book *(Drill Press, 3:AM Magazine's Non-Fiction Book of the Year 2009). His next novel, with secret title and hidden nature, illustrated by the alchemical artist David Aronson, is coming next year from the occult publisher,* Mandrake of Oxford. *Further curiosity can be indulged at* tombradley. org.

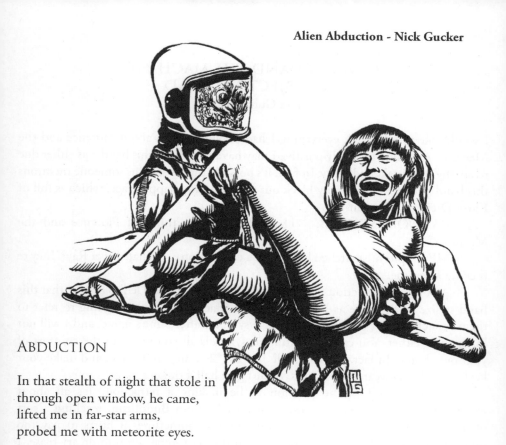

ABDUCTION

In that stealth of night that stole in
through open window, he came,
lifted me in far-star arms,
probed me with meteorite eyes.

I yelled. I was weightless to him,
zero gravity: my face, my breasts
floating up. That terrible smile
inside his mask chilled me

with its familiarity. Here was
a deadly visitor whose chest
I had slept against. I knew him
like I knew my father. And then

the lights came on, cameras stopped.
Polystyrene coffee cups circled
like cheap satellites in lazy orbits.
He looked so normal. I could've screamed.

Adam Lowe

FLORENCE AND THE MACHINE
ARE OBJECTIVELY BAD
Jess Gulbranson

I would like to take back everything I had previously said about Florence and the Machine. Anything remotely positive I may have said about this band was either due to apathy or mistaken identity. In fact, it's possible that as soon as someone mentions this band to me, I temporarily black out and go to my happy place, which is full of Karin Dreijer Andersson.

RANDOM SCHLUB: "Hey, what do you think of Florence and the Machine?"

ME (pupils mismatched like I have a concussion): "What? Fever Ray? They're fucking awesome."

A point of distinction must be made at this point. I am led to believe that this band stylizes their name as "Florence + The Machine." I am not going to refer to them as such. I don't type out the garbage symbols after Sunn's name, and I will not budge here either. You can use gratuitous symbols all you want, in the comfort of your own home. In fact, you can spell "to" as "2" , dress in purple, and make your keyboard players wear assless pants. I don't give half a tinker's fuck.

So why am I in the position to be making a retraction? It's all about mindfulness. That is a general lesson that I take from Buddhism, reaching a sort of deadly sharpness in my career as music critic. Sometimes it hurts to pay too much attention, and anyone can be forgiven the occasional slip into dreary blase. I can recall the aforementioned random schlubs asking about them, and I know I've sorted through a million album submissions that mention them as an influence, and it seems like all my friends who are moms were posting on Facebook about how nice it was to listen to them with the family.

As I intimated earlier, I believe a critic should never succumb to "Um, okay." A critic should be a stepping razor. Smokestack lightning. So yes, I must retract everything I had said about Florence and the Machine.

I dread continuing, because to prep for this piece I had to listen to a lot of FatM. A lot, and I really couldn't hack it. My stomach—I kid you not—started churning after I looked at Florence Welch's pained attempts at ritualistic pantomime and soulful band leadership. Urgh. But I will continue. All the Patriarchs will look upon my endeavor with pride.

There are a lot of shocking discoveries to be made when listening to the radio. In this case, my wife and I were driving to work and a song came on. At first my interest was piqued. "Who is that?" Then I listened to it, and my impression of a sort of half-assed ripoff of Loreena Mckennit crystallized into sheer hatred. It was the most miserable pile of cliches I'd ever heard, backed by a sloppy arrangement that had a certain cloying familiarity.

Hmm. Where had I heard this kind of crap before? Oh yes, I remember. Megachurch worship bands. And I know megachurch worship bands—I was in one. But that's a story for another time.

I'm sure by now you're wondering what song this was that could inspire such an extreme reaction in an ordinarily mild-mannered gent like myself. Well, wonder no longer—it was "Shake It Out" by good ol' Florence and her terrible Machine. In case you've never experienced this dainty little turd, let me share some of the choice lyrical gems with you.

> And I'm damned if I do and I'm damned if I don't
> So here's to drinks in the dark at the end of my road
> And I'm ready to suffer and I'm ready to hope
> It's a shot in the dark aimed right at my throat
> 'Cause looking for heaven, found the devil in me
> Looking for heaven, found the devil in me
> Well what the hell I'm gonna let it happen to me, yeah

Fuck me. I don't even have words for that. No, wait, I do. "Hackneyed." "Vapid." "End it all." Lest I be accused of reading too much—or too little—into these lyrics, let's give Florence some rope and let her finish the job:

> I was thinking of regrets, like, you know when you feel like you're stuck in yourself, you keep repeating certain patterns of behavior, and you kind of want to cut out that part of you and restart yourself. [. . .] So this song was kind of like, 'Shake yourself out of it, things will be OK.'

Yes, Florence, indeed. For a minute there I was starting to doubt your commitment to Sparkle Motion.

"Wait a darn minute, Jess," you're saying. "You miserable bastard. You can't judge a band by just one of their soulful well-crafted pop hits!" Actually, I can and do. And you, my dear vosotros, are colectively a stupid fuck. Please let me finish.

Okay, I suppose it's only fair to go the extra mile. If there's one thing I believe, it's that critics are objectively right and the average passive consumer is objectively wrong. So with a bit of noblesse oblige, I will justify my assessment. I'm doing this for you. Don't forget that.

I started with a headache before I wrote this, and now that I have listened to a baker's dozen of this pap, migraine has gone to a serious desire to crawl into the peace and safety of a new dark age, preferably by way of jumping into a chemical fire and dying. Let's continue, but quickly. There is a bottle of Jameson and an Ernest Hemingway novel waiting for me.

"Drumming Song"—This track, I'm guessing, has consciously aped Bjork's earlier work for its intro, before it goes full Algernon and sounds like every other FatM song. In fact, that is emerging as a common thread in their music—a reasonably dynamic opening with a prominent vocal, that then is submerged in a slurry of generic instrumentation and backing vocals that are simultaneously busy and blurry. The video features what I am guessing is supposed to be an African tribesman dancing, and the message I get from that is "The song is about drumming, and black people have rhythm, so . . . " Well, fuck you, Florence. You racist bitch.

"Cosmic Love"—Hey, look, the standard opening arps and harps and Florence's vocals, and then it kicks into shit overdrive. Did I mention there are more tepid lyrics? No? Well, there are.

"Breath of Life"—The last one made me want to go listen to "Cosmic Hug" by Fareed Haque, and this makes me want to go listen to "Kiss of Life" by Peter Gabriel. You know, good music. This one is tricky—there's a sort of percussion movement at the beginning before the standard opening yet again. I will say that this song has a little edge to it, as far as the actual music, but it's still burdened by the sloppy multipartite vocals and New Age lyrical nonsense.

"No Light, No Light"—I fucking wish. All these songs are starting to sound the same, or maybe my brain function is failing. Thank goodness. I wonder what it's like to be a musician on one of these sessions. That doesn't sound like something I could handle. But seriously, I have seen the output of random song lyric generators, and this is pretty much it. You know, the computer asks you what you're into, you tell it "roses, heaven, twilight, demons, souls, lace,"| and it shits out a Florence and the Machine song. True story!

"Rabbit Heart"—Here I think the dark, um, heart of the matter has become plain. There is not much I can say about the song itself, because it is the same old crap, but the video speaks volumes. Yes, I understand that some might think I am paying more attention to the videos than strictly necessary, but I am a cold hearted snake of the old school. The Frankfurt School, to be specific, and I believe that there is a social context for every work of art that cannot be denied. In this case I feel that Florence is exorcising some living paper doll frustrations, dancing about in costume and inflicting her terrible teenage poetry on an adoring audience. She must love it when people compare her to Kate Bush or Bjork or whatever.

Oh, I hear you piping up again. "Jess, Jess, you jackass. You already namechecked Fever Ray and Peter Gabriel, so, um, something about costumes. Gotcha!" Let me say this again: Fuck. You. The difference between Florence and the

Machine versus Pete and Karin is that the latter two don't suck. Lyrics don't have to make sense, they don't have to spell anything out specifically, but they do need to have some sort of verisimilitude or hidden layers. That's the reason Morrissey is awesome, while Colin Meloy is not. The Decemberists have songs that don't sound like the lyricists have ever lived their life, and Florence and the Machine have that identical problem in spades.

What's the verdict, then? I am a proponent of liking what you like, and not being ashamed of it. Discovering that I was able to enjoy things without irony, without them being a guilty pleasure, is one of the formative experiences in my life as both artist and critic. So how can that jibe with the vitriol I've been slinging so far? Well, hey you can listen to Florence and the Machine if you like them.

You'll just be dead fucking wrong.

Tune in next time, when I dissect The Killers' "Battle Born", and take time out of my review to shit on The Clash for no good reason.

Jess Gulbranson is the author of novels 10 A BOOT STOMPING 20 A HUMAN FACE 30 GOTO 10, Mel, *and* Antipaladin Blues. *His short fiction, poetry, and art have been featured in* Lambshead's Cabinet, Kizuna, Umbrella Journal, *and* Bradley Sands is a Dick. *For* Crappy Indie Music: The Blog *he is a critic, interviewer, and douchebag-in-residence. Jess makes music under the names Coeur Machant and DJ Falsifier. He lives in Portland with his wife and daughter.*

ABOUT THE ARTISTS

Front Cover—*Matthew Revert resides in Melbourne, Australia, which makes him Australian. He is in charge of the Spontaneous Vox Pop Society and has just completed a successful season of trouser-related questions.* matthewrevert. com

Author Of The Species p7—*Nick Patterson is a visual artist whose love of twisting minds and turning heads has led him to explore all the darkness the human experience can muster, through high contrast ink drawings. With no official training in the visual medium, Patterson's art is loosely tethered to reality, although it is very detailed. His inspiration is drawn from an amalgam of cartoons, comics, and movies. Carrying a sketchbook with him everywhere, he lets no flicker of imagination escape. Nick Patterson's art has been published in several small magazines and novels. He currently lives in a city full of flowers on the western edge of Canada.* (nickdjp.com)

Wiggly Fetus p12, **Many Madonas** p46—*Alan M. Clark grew up in Tennessee in a house full of bones and old medical books. His illustrations have appeared in books of fiction, non-fiction, textbooks, young adult fiction and children's books. Awards for his illustration work include the World Fantasy Award and four Chesley Awards. His short fiction has appeared in magazines and anthologies and five of his novels have been published. Lazy Fascist Press will release his sixth novel,* A Parliament of Crows, *in the Fall of 2012. Mr Clark's publishing company, IFD Publishing, has released six traditional books and sixteen ebooks. He and his wife, Melody, live in Oregon.* alanmclark.com

Function p35-39—*Vikki Hastings is a young artist from Scotland. She has contributed to many exhibitions and publications, most recently issue 9 of* Polluto *magazine.*

Mayor Nimble Makes It Known p32—*Steve Aylett* first appeared in *Alan Moore's* Dodgem Logic *magazine. Steve Aylett is an award nominated slipstream/sci-fi author who's comic book credits include,* The Nerve *and* Johnny Viable. *His latest novel* Novahead *is* available from all good retailers.

Penmanship p52—*David Aronson lives and works in the Philadelphia area. His quirky, offbeat drawings, paintings and illustration combine traditional media such as watercolor, ink, graphite and colored pencil with digital media*

and digital collage. His work ranges from whimsical to fantastic, from highly stylized to realistically rendered, and has been called unique and highly imaginative. It mixes lowbrow with fine art elements and often employs unusual juxtapositions. Thematically, David often delves into the realms of mythology and psychology. He has created art for CD covers, music videos, magazines, books, music posters and tour t-shirts. David is also an oil painter and has completed several public and private commissions. His digital animation has been featured on MTV2 and Fuse and his drawings and illustrations have appeared in Silkmilk, Ritual, Inside Artzine, Khooligan, Fugue *and* BigNews, *as well as being exhibited nationally in galleries and museum shows. His work has been featured in a college level illustration textbook, the book* The Immanence of Myth *and most recently in the anthology* Dark Stories By Dark Artists *from Cypi Press. He is an art teacher, working with both children and adults and teaching several different media, and was once the sole owner and operator of a small art school in the Philadelphia suburbs. He is also a certified hypnotherapist, professional astrologer, and published poet. David's work can be seen online at* alchemicalwedding.com.

Alien Abduction p58—Nick Gucker *When he's not busy whispering to insects, trying his hand at taxidermy or watching weird Japanese monster movies Nick Gucker can be found hunched over his art table dreaming up disturbing nightmares and freakish delights.*

His art has appeared in the pages of Strange Aeons Magazine *and* The Magazine of Bizarro Fiction. *His illustrations have decorated the pages of* ALL-MONSTER ACTION! *by Cody Goodfellow, the novelette "The Eye of Infinity" by David Conyers for Perilous Press,* The Aklonoimicon *anthology from Aklo Press, a re-issue of H. P. Lovecraft's "Under the Pyramids", as well as book covers for Blysster Press authors Clyde Wolfe, R. L. Reeves, M. R. Mitchell and the 2011 and 2012 "De-Compostions" horror anthologies. His artistic contributions can be found in online publications including Lovecraftzine.com and Thisishorror.co.uk. His unique, one-of-a-kind custom commission pieces have graced the walls and limbs of various and sundry patrons of the arts.*

Back Cover (Piercings)—*Justin T Coons is a freelance artist/illustrator from outside of Philadelphia, PA. He specializes in horror, bizarro and pinup artwork. Visit him on Facebook for additional information.* facebook.com/horrorart

ND - #0036 - 270225 - C8 - 234/156/4 - PB - 9781907133497 - Matt Lamination